SALFORD QUAYS
THE STORY OF MANCHESTER D

EDWARD GRAY

C000245176

A *Memories* Publication

Published by:
Memories
222 Kings Road
Stretford
Trafford
M16 03Q

ISBN 1 899181 88 1
©Edward Gray

Series Editor

Cliff Hayes

Printed by
MFP Design and Print
Longford Trading Estate,
Thomas Street, Stretford,
Manchester. M16 0JA
Tel:0161 864 4540 Fax:0161 866 9866

Salford Docks in the boom years of the early 1960s. The tongue of land in the centre is now the location of The Lowry Centre. To the left, crowded with shipping, is the former Number 9 Dock, and to the right are former docks 8,7,and 6. To commemorate the former trading links with Canada, the water basins have been named after the Great Lakes, Ontario, Huron, and Erie. At the head and to the west side of the large dock, commercial developments have been named Anchorage and Harbour City respectively. In the foreground is Trafford Wharf, now Quay West, soon to be home of the northern branch of the Imperial War Museum, and now linked to the opposite bank by a new lifting footbridge. (Airviews)

CONTENTS

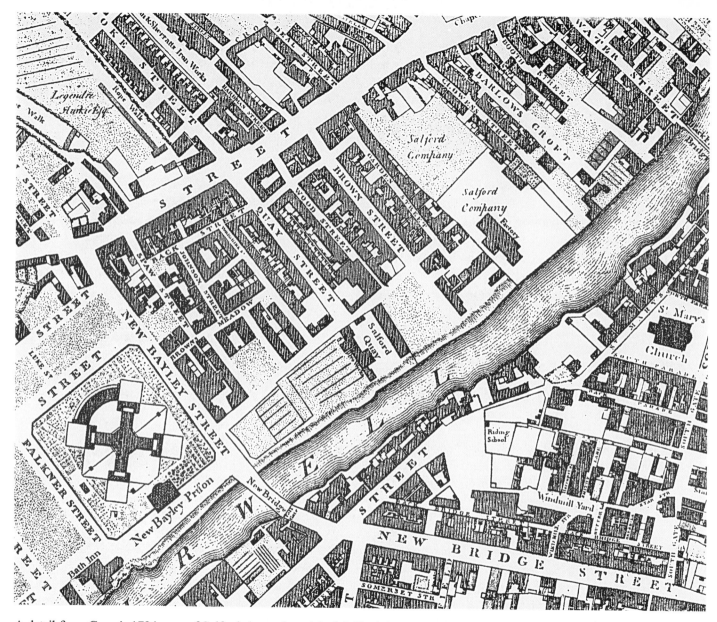

A detail from Green's 1794 map of Salford shows the original Salford Quay located between the New Bayley Street toll bridge and Blackfriars Bridge. The Salford Quay Company was a major carrier on the old river navigation, rivalling the Duke of Bridgewater's enterprise, so much so that he purchased shares and by 1779 had become the sole owner of the Company. Salford's own Quay Street leads off from Chapel Street to the river. Blackfriars Street was at that time named Water Street. (Salford Local History Library)

INTRODUCTION

In the mid-1700s the original Salford Quay was to be found not in the present Salford Quays location, but on the northern bank of the River Irwell, that natural boundary between Salford and Manchester, in the area of land which lies between Blackfriars and New Bailey Street bridges. This stretch of the Irwell was the limit of the old river navigation, and here along the banks were established the wharves and warehouses of the trading companies which carried the raw materials and finished goods of this developing commercial region. On the Salford side, between Chapel Street and the river, there still exists a Quay Street, not as well-known as Manchester's Quay Street on the opposite bank, but, nevertheless, having its origins in that same period of the eighteenth century when trade was blossoming and when local traders sought to establish improved facilities for the carriage of goods by water.

Until that time, the commercial traffic of Lancashire had depended for imported supplies on barge navigation on the tidal reaches of the Mersey, and overland carriage of goods by pack-horse on unmade and sometimes impassable roads. Late in the seventeenth century, Thomas Patten, a wealthy merchant, had cleared obstructions in the river estuary to allow vessels to reach Bank Quay, Warrington, and had suggested that an extension of this work, by dredging and deepening the rivers Mersey and Irwell, might enable vessels to proceed as far as Manchester. After a survey of 1712, promoters formed the Mersey & Irwell Navigation Company, but progress was slow, and not until 1721 was the Act gained enabling work to commence. Even then, it was some considerable time, probably about 1734, before vessels of a modest size could reach 'Salford Key,' as it was then named. The sailing 'flats' were shallow-draught boats, which could work on the Mersey estuary as well as on the rivers. It was usual for the 'flats' to sail up the estuary from Liverpool on the high tide and enter the river system at Howley Lock, Warrington. The Company's source of income was the tolls charged for the carriage of goods (maximum three shillings and fourpence per ton), in return for which the Company maintained the river navigation in good order. Soon, it was estimated that there were 20 sailing 'flats' regularly engaged in working from Liverpool to the 'Salford Key' or to the wharves on the Manchester side. Carriage by water was less expensive than by land, but the river system suffered from the problems of floods on the one hand, and droughts on the other. Consequently, merchants remained uncertain about the reliability of the river traffic, and in its early years the Mersey & Irwell system did not make a profit.

The extension of the Duke of Bridgewater's canal to Runcorn in 1776 offered an alternative and more reliable connection to the Mersey Estuary. The monopoly of the river navigation was thus broken, though, despite competition from the new railways, trade was increasing and there seemed to be sufficient traffic for the two systems to share. The Bridgewater Trustees became owners of both waterways in 1844, at a period when dissatisfaction was running high over costly railway rates and allegedly extortionate port dues charged by Liverpool on goods passing through its docks. Proposals for the construction of a wider and deeper waterway to Manchester had been made earlier, one of which in 1840 sought to improve and enlarge the Mersey & Irwell river system, but this was the period when funds were being poured into railway construction, and finance for waterway schemes was not so easily obtained. In fact, the Bridgewater Trustees allowed the river navigation to deteriorate, preferring to invest money in keeping the canal in good condition, and regarding the river system as merely a secondary stand-by to be used if repairs were needed on the canal. In 1876 a letter from George Hicks of the Manchester Chamber of Commerce waterway schemes was not so easily obtained. In fact, the Bridgewater Trustees allowed the river navigation to deteriorate, preferring to invest money in keeping the canal in good condition, and regarding the river system as merely a secondary stand-by to be used if repairs were needed on the canal. In 1876 a letter from George Hicks of the Manchester Chamber of Commerce was published in the 'Manchester Guardian' and re-opened the debate. Hicks lamented the neglected state of the river navigation and suggested once again the construction of a 'ship canal' in order to avoid paying railway rates, trans-shipment costs, and port dues at Liverpool.

Opinion moved in favour of such a scheme, for lower transport costs were vital if the region's products were to become cheaper and more competitive. Cotton spinners claimed that raw material could be purchased on the Continent, brought in via east coast ports and transported to Manchester by rail, and still make a saving on the cost of importing it through Liverpool. Exporters complained that over half the cost of sending out their products was eaten up by railway and dock charges before the goods had left Liverpool. In 1882 Daniel Adamson, owner of a Dukinfield engineering firm, called a meeting which set the ship canal scheme in motion. He invited 55 merchants and manufacturers, together with civic officials representing thirteen Lancashire towns, to his home in Didsbury. As a result, the scheme for the conversion of the river system was born. The plans of Edward Leader Williams were deemed most feasible and the first proposals were submitted to Parliament in 1883. Opponents included the railways, the Liverpool port authorities, and the Bridgewater Navigation Company, which countered with its own proposals to improve the river system. Approval was not gained until the third attempt in the Bill of 1885, when the plan had been amended to extend the ship canal along the Cheshire banks of the Mersey instead of dredging a channel in the middle of the estuary. The Act included the proviso that the river navigation must be purchased, and the Bridgewater Canal kept in good condition for all who wished to use it. The two waterways were purchased in August 1887 for £1,710,000, the highest amount presented on a cheque up to that time. In the five years which had elapsed since Daniel Adamson's 1882 meeting, an additional half-million pounds had been spent in gaining Parliamentary approval and it remained necessary to raise a further five million pounds before work began in November 1887. Adamson resigned from his position as Chairman because of differences of opinion over fund-raising matters, and, sadly, did not live to see the completion of the project he had initiated. He died in 1890, aged 71. In the following year, the Canal began to open in sections, starting from the estuary end. Ships were able to use the Canal to reach Ellesmere Port and the Weaver Navigation in 1891. The Runcorn length was ready in 1893, and in the same year the last portions of land were released for the final excavations to take place. These were at places where railway routes crossed the course of the Canal, and where the original lines had been left in place whilst the long deviation embankments to raise the tracks over the waterway had been built and properly tested. The Canal was filled from end to end in November 1893, and opened for traffic on New Year's Day, 1st January 1894.

The construction of the Ship Canal brought great economic benefits to the region. Tonnage grew annually, reaching peak years in the 1950s. Thereafter, changes in local manufacturing industries, shifts in the patterns of trade, and increasing competition on North Atlantic shipping routes, followed by mergers and take-over bids in the 1970s, all combined to cause a decline in the market for cargo handling services. Ocean-going container ships and tankers grew to such a size as could not be accommodated in the locks of the Canal. By the early 1980s, although the seaward end of the Canal remained busy, shippers were reluctant to commit vessels to the extra journey time required to sail the 36 miles to Salford, and traffic fell to such an extent that the Canal Company lost revenue and seriously considered closing the upper reaches altogether. However, as the Canal moved into its second century, the imaginative scheme for the re-development of the former docklands was implemented, and has led to the transformation of the Salford Quays area into an attractive mixture of private residential, commercial, and leisure interests, to which is now added the prestigious Lowry gallery and theatre complex, with the northern branch of the Imperial War Museum yet to be completed on Trafford Wharf. A very different picture from 1894 !

CHAPTER 1

THE FIRST SALFORD QUAY, NAVIGATION ON THE IRWELL AND THE PLAN FOR A SHIP CANAL

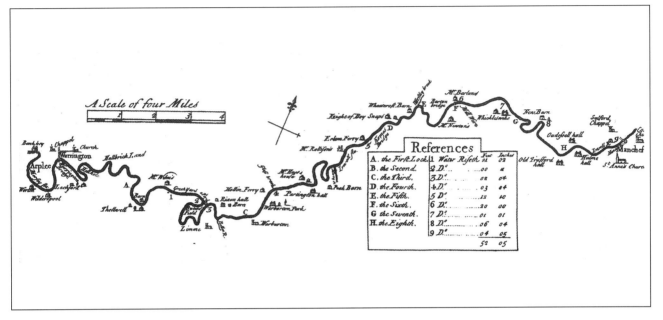

In a survey commissioned *"by order of the Gentlemen at Manchester"* in 1712 Thomas Steers, who had been responsible for the construction of docks at Liverpool, reported on the feasibility of making the rivers Mersey and Irwell navigable as far Manchester. The survey recorded that some locks and weirs already existed on the rivers. Steers proposed the construction, or reconstruction, of eight weirs in order to maintain a good depth of water along the whole course, each weir to be by-passed by a lock to lift the vessels to the higher water upstream. Because of the winding nature of the rivers, the boats' sails would be of only limited use. The work of hauling the boats upstream would have to be done by horses or men, so the recommendations included the construction of a tow-path along the whole of the route. The object of the scheme was said to be the more favourable movement of *"valuable manufactures in woollen, linen, and cotton"* from both Lancashire and Yorkshire and the better carriage of *"groceries, dying stuff, and other imported goods."* Refinements of the scheme would include straightening some winding parts of the course or making *'cuts'* (short canals) across meanders to reduce the total distance.

The work of new lock construction and the clearing and dredging of the 22 miles of river upstream from Warrington was slow, and it was not until about 1734 that boats could reach the terminal wharves at Manchester. Along the inland length of the navigation, the final three locks were constructed at Barton, Mode Wheel, and Throstle Nest, the latter being the last rise before the head of navigation at the original Salford Quay, downstream of the present Victoria Bridge. At all these three points, as at several locations elsewhere further downstream, the interests of long-established corn mills were protected by a special clause in the Act. At Barton, a weir and mill-race provided the force to turn the water wheel of Bardsley's mill, on the Trafford Park bank. The towpath and lock were on the northern bank. The approach to the lock, enabling vessels to negotiate the obstacle of the weir and rise to the higher water beyond, may be seen in the foreground of this 1888 picture. (The Barton Locks of the 1894 Ship Canal were constructed approximately one mile downstream to the west of the original river locks.)

The Duke of Bridgewater's canal from Worsley to Manchester crossed the river navigation at Barton in 1761. The view downstream, looking in the opposite direction from the previous illustration, shows Brindley's stone aqueduct as constructed over the waterway close to the approach to the lock. When the Duke's canal was extended to Runcorn in 1776, it offered a more reliable connection from Manchester's Castlefield area (not many yards from the terminal wharves of the river navigation) to the Mersey estuary and Liverpool. The 22-year monopoly of the Mersey & Irwell Company was thus broken. The impact of the canal route was immediate, and the Company offered to sell their river navigation to the Duke, an offer he declined. However, new directors initiated improvements on the river system, and with the rising canal mania of the early nineteenth century, the two navigations became friendly rivals.

The corn millers did not welcome the disruption caused by the reconstruction of locks and weirs, though they made use of the river navigation to bring in raw materials and to carry away their products. The lowering of water levels when mill-owners allowed too much water to escape through the mill-races was often a source of conflict with the bargemen. At Mode Wheel, a place-name derived from the title 'Maud's Wheel' (the wheels were often given ladies' names), the flour mill on the Salford bank also crushed logwood for the manufacture of dyes for the textile industry. The lock lay alongside the mill. Originally, the locks were some 13 feet wide, but all seem to have been reconstructed at a later date to accommodate somewhat larger vessels. The dimensions of the locks governed the size of the sailing flats which could be used on the waterway - a dilemma which was to surface again a century or more later in the much larger 65 feet-wide locks of the Ship Canal. (MSCCo)

A few yards upstream from Mode Wheel Lock, an arched bridge carried the towpath across a channel which gave access to a mooring basin behind the mill. Beyond the bridge was the lock-keeper's cottage, with the towpath continuing in the direction of Manchester towards the next and final lock at Throstle Nest. (The original Mode Wheel Locks of the river navigation were a short distance to the north-west of the later Ship Canal locks, and in this picture the photographer was pointing his camera towards the future site of the main terminal docks in Salford, now known as 'Salford Quays.'

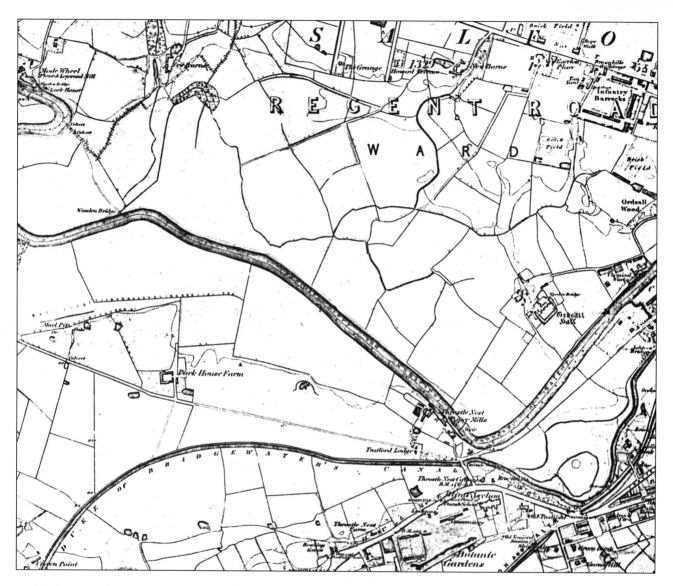

Until the latter part of the nineteenth century, the Ordsall area of Salford remained largely rural. In this mid-nineteenth century map, Mode Wheel Locks lie top left, giving access to the stretch of river before the final rise at Throstle Nest Lock and paper mills. The river navigation continued to be improved even as late as 1878, when a new cut was made across the meander at Mode Wheel. As the movement to convert the river system into a major ship canal gained momentum, this area of Salford became the prospective site for the new terminal docks. The sharp bend in the river at Throstle Nest was to become the location of the Trafford Road Swing Bridge.

The furthest inland of the river locks, Throstle Nest Lock was located on the Old Trafford bank, and lifted vessels into the last stretch of the river before Manchester. In this 1888 view, during what must have been the last few months of operation, two narrow boats lashed side-by-side are approaching the lock, apparently sharing a sail. The whitewashed lock-keeper's cottage has a built-on vantage point, enabling him to observe approaching vessels in both directions, not unlike the toll-gate houses on turnpike roads. In the early years of the river navigation, boat crews had been trusted to operate the lock gates, but in 1806, partly as a result of the increasing number of vessels and partly because of damage to gates, keepers were employed, and small cottages to house them were built alongside the locks. Because navigation of the river continued into the hours of darkness, lock-keepers had to be available at all times. In the foreground, there are signs of things to come - the fencing and temporary railway embankment indicate that the contractor for the Ship Canal project is about to commence work. (MSCCo/GMCRO)

The landing stage by Albert Bridge, New Bailey Street, was at one time said to be the busiest spot on the river. From 1807, before the days of the railway, the Mersey & Irwell Company offered a passenger service along the river navigation, competing with a similar provision on the Bridgewater Canal. From this point on the Salford bank, passenger boats departed at 8.00 a.m. each day, reaching Runcorn at 4.00 p.m. In the other direction, a boat left Runcorn at 8.00 a.m. in summer, 10.00 a.m. in winter, also taking eight hours on the journey. The boats connected with various stage coach services en route, and would stop at any of the riverside wharves as required. From Runcorn passengers could travel on larger vessels across the estuary to Liverpool, a service on which steamships were introduced in 1816. The introduction of much faster railway services after the opening of the Liverpool & Manchester Railway in 1830 greatly affected passenger traffic on the river, and the packet-boats were withdrawn in the 1860s. Some local pleasure services remained, however. Sailings to Pomona Gardens were popular on summer days, and in 1894, when the Ship Canal was still a novelty, steamers such as these carried people to view the docks. The landing stage survives at the side of what is now the *'Mark Addy'* public house, and the original stonework can be seen. Even today, the pleasure boat *'Princess Katherine'* departs from this spot for tours of Salford Quays. The original *'Salford Key,'* terminus of the river navigation, lay beyond the bridge.

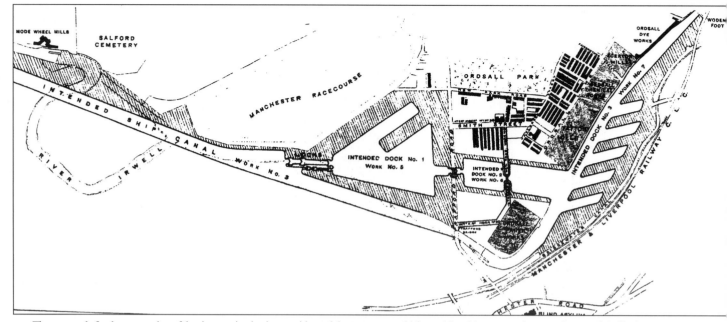

The proposals for the conversion of the river navigation into a wider and deeper system which would enable ocean-going vessels to reach Salford, sprang from the dissatisfaction of local traders with the high railway rates and excessive port dues levied on goods passing through Liverpool. The original proposals for the terminal docks in Salford were embodied in an 1885 plan, which envisaged a large triangular dock located between the Racecourse and the river, opposite to the Trafford Park estate. This would have been entered via locks from the main canal, connected to another dock in the Ordsall area of Salford, and would have led on to five smaller docks at Pomona, beyond Throstle Nest lock. (From Bosdin Leech)

The rural nature of the area around Mode Wheel is typified by this 1890 picture of the cobbled lane leading to Mode Wheel flour mill.

The success of the Suez Canal, opened in 1869, had encouraged promoters of the Manchester Ship Canal scheme to think in terms of the largest vessels of the day. It was resolved that any ship of a size which could pass through Suez must also be able to get to Manchester. Consequently, the minimum depth of the projected 36-mile Ship Canal was to be 26 feet (the same as Suez, but later increased to 28 feet by raising the water level), and the minimum bottom width was to be 120 feet, allowing large vessels to pass each other. After Parliamentary permission had been gained at the third attempt in 1885, there followed an intense period of fund-raising, land purchase negotiations, and the acquisition of the Bridgewater Navigation. The Bridgewater Canal was to be kept intact, but the river navigation would inevitably be destroyed in the construction of the Ship Canal. As a result, work did not commence until November 1887. It was estimated it would take four-and-a-half years to complete. Excavated material was used to form long embankments for railway deviations, for at five points where existing lines crossed the course, tracks had to be lifted to 75 feet above the canal surface. Spoil was also used to fill up the old beds of the rivers, and to raise low lands near the canal. Work was carried out *'in the dry'* by allowing river water to flow in original or diverted channels until the time came for it to be admitted into sections of the finished canal. The scale of the excavations may be gauged by this view of a group of navvies taking a rest break. The contractor's locomotive *'SULLY'* stands with a train of empty spoil wagons on temporary track in the base of the workings. In the background, sections of the bank have been faced. (Salford Museums & Heritage Services)

14. The total work force employed on the construction of the Ship Canal numbered some 17,000, and the bulk of the excavation was done by 80 *'steam-navvies'* and *'land dredgers.'* For the conveyance of materials and the removal of spoil, 173 steam locomotives and and 6300 wagons worked along 228 miles of temporary track. To enable work to commence simultaneously along the length of the canal, the course was divided into eight sections, with a resident engineer appointed to each. At the Salford end, the original Section 8 (Barton to Woden Street, Hulme) was considered to be the most important length of the canal, for it included the locks at Barton and Mode Wheel, the Bridgewater Canal swing aqueduct, two swing road bridges, and the whole of the terminal docks. It is recorded that on this section alone 2800 men were employed, along with 26 horses, 30 locomotives, 7 steam navvies, 3 cranes, and 7 excavators. So heavy was the work on this section, that it was subsequently sub-divided, with Section 9 taking dock work only. The 1887 Hunslet locomotive *'Irwell'* was one of many purchased by T.A.Walker specifically for the Ship Canal contract, most of which were given names of local places or features along the course of the workings. During the construction period, engine drivers were often referred to as *'navvy crackers.'* (Salford Museums & Heritage Services)

The plans for the terminal docks were amended in 1890 after arrangements with the Trafford Estate. Sir Humphrey de Trafford had been an implacable opponent of the Ship Canal scheme, so much so that he had insisted the Company must build a nine-feet-high wall between the canal and his estate in order to protect his privacy. After his death in 1886, however, negotiations had re-opened with his sucessor (eldest son Humphrey Francis) who agreed to sell to the Company a portion of the Trafford Park estate, a length of water frontage which became Trafford Wharf. The revised layout shows the planned route of the canal in relation to the former course of the river. The 1878 *'cut'* made at a relatively late stage in the life of the river navigation to shorten the distance across the Irwell meander at Mode Wheel may be noted. The revised plans involved the transfer of some 40 acres of land from Stretford to the Salford side of the waterway,

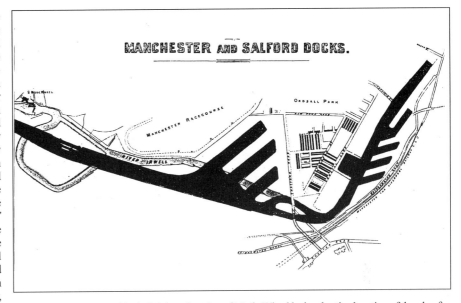

MANCHESTER AND SALFORD DOCKS.

an arrangement made not without considerable municipal wrangling, and included the relocation of Mode Wheel locks, drastic alteration of the plan for a triangular dock by the racecourse, a widening of the channel up to Trafford Bridge, and the abandonment of the intention to create large docks by Ordsall Lane. Note the division of the river at Trafford Bridge. (From Bosdin Leech)

The plans for the terminal docks included a large water area for a turning basin to enable ships to be swung aroung before commencing their return journey down the canal. An unusual feature of the construction work in Salford was the erection in the basin of two dredgers (the *'Irk'* and *'Medlock'*) manufactured by the firm of Fleming and Ferguson. The dredgers had been transported from Paisley in sections and were erected on site. In March 1893, when the dock excavations were ready for the admittance of water, the dredgers were floated from their stocks, and the *'Medlock'* ate its way out by cutting away the dam which divided the docks from the canal proper.

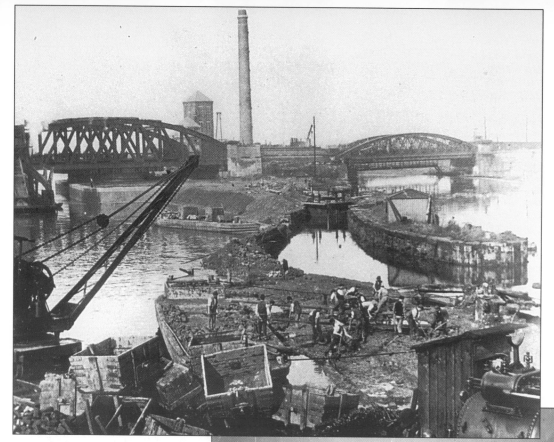

The Mersey & Irwell river navigation was inevitably destroyed in the construction of the Ship Canal. The old locks at Throstle Nest are here seen in 1893 during the last stages of the work on the final section to Pomona. The Trafford Road swing bridge is already in place on the left. Originally, the river flowed beneath the fixed bridge to the right, until diverted by the cutting of the Ship Canal. For a time both bridges existed together, but the watercourse under the fixed bridge was afterwards filled in to serve as an access route for Ship Canal railway sidings. The tubs in the foreground were used to carry away spoil and debris during the demolition of the locks. (MSCCo/GMCRO)

At less important road crossing points, the Canal Company provided swing bridges of a similar pattern but narrower than at Trafford Road. Barton Road Bridge was typical of the smaller type of bridge. Bridgemen closed the gates across the roads before bridges were swung. The spherical baskets on the poles were raised or lowered by ropes, and before the days of radio communication, the position of the baskets indicated to the ships' masters or pilots whether or not they had permission to proceed. The swing aqueduct which carries the Bridgewater Canal over the Ship Canal at Barton is off the picture to the right.

CHAPTER 2

THE EARLY YEARS OF THE SHIP CANAL
1894-1905

The full length of the Canal opened for traffic on the 1st January 1894, amid great rejoicing. A procession of 71 ships, led by Samuel Platt's steam yacht *'Norseman,'* sailed from Latchford to the terminal docks. Over 50,000 tickets had been printed for spectators to watch the arrivals in Salford. Many of the vessels in the procession carried directors, councillors, and invited guests, but there were also several cargo ships in the inaugural voyage. The steamship *'Pioneer,'* owned by the Co-operative Wholesale Society, brought in and unloaded a cargo of sugar on that first day. She also claimed the distinction of being the first vessel to be registered in the Port of Manchester. A second opening ceremony took place on the 21st May 1894, when Queen Victoria (who had arrived by train) boarded the royal yacht *'Enchantress'* at Trafford Wharf, declared the waterway officially open, and conferred knighthoods on the mayors of Manchester and Salford. The Queen returned to the railway station in an open carriage by way of Trafford Road and Regent Road, where she passed beneath this triumphal arch.

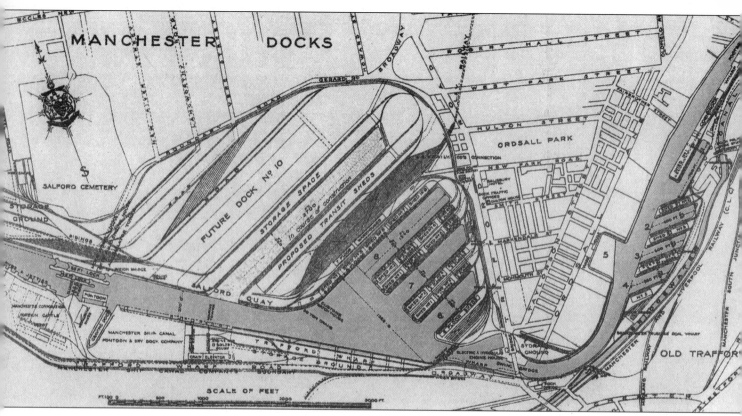

The plans for the terminal docks as amended after the purchase of Trafford Wharf showed several alterations from the original scheme. The four small docks, numbered 1 to 4, on the Old Trafford bank at Pomona were retained, but the scheme for Dock number 5 on the opposite side, which would have been alongside Goodwin's Ivy Soap Works, was dropped. In fact, there was never a Number 5 Dock. The larger docks for ocean-going ships, numbers 6, 7 and 8, were completed as planned to the west of Trafford Road, and Trafford Wharf became the location of a grain elevator, a timber storage ground, dry dock repair facilities, and a foreign cattle wharf. Negotiations began early for the purchase of the racecourse site, where No.9 Dock is optimistically shown as "in course of construction" in 1898, though the last race meeting there was not held until 1901. Even more optimistically, the site of 'FUTURE DOCK No. 10' is outlined alongside, although this was never built. (From Bosdin Leech)

The Trafford Road Bridge was the largest, heaviest, and busiest of the seven swing road bridges along the course of the Canal, but being the furthest inland, it was the least busy in terms of shipping movements. Passing through to reach the small docks at Pomona is the Fisher Renwick steamer, 'Lancer,' one of several vessels employed by this Newcastle shipping line on the regular coastal service between Manchester and London. (Charles Downs)

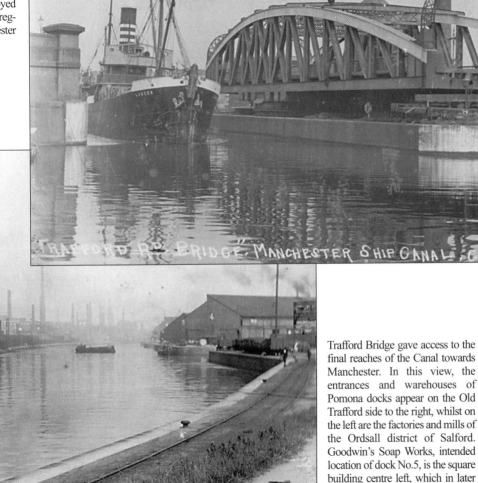

Trafford Bridge gave access to the final reaches of the Canal towards Manchester. In this view, the entrances and warehouses of Pomona docks appear on the Old Trafford side to the right, whilst on the left are the factories and mills of the Ordsall district of Salford. Goodwin's Soap Works, intended location of dock No.5, is the square building centre left, which in later years became part of the Colgate Palmolive group. Both banks of the Canal enjoyed railway access. (Commercial postcard)

Dock No.1 at Pomona was the only one which lay partly within the Manchester city boundary. All the others were in either Stretford or Salford. All docks were equipped with transit sheds for storage, receipt and dispatch of cargoes, and some open wharves at Pomona specialised in handling bulk cargoes, particularly sand, gravel, etc. for the building trades. (Barrett & Co.)

The Fisher Renwick steamers became regular visitors to Pomona Docks, easily recognisable by their funnel markings of three narrow white bands. Most of the line's vessels were given military titles (such as 'Trooper,' 'Fusilier,' 'Lancer'), but this one carried the name 'Fishren,' made up of the first two parts of the surnames of the Company's founders. Sadly, this particular vessel was lost after a collision off Dover in 1906. The barge alongside was receiving barrels for onward transmission, possibly via connections to the narrow boat canals.

SS. FISHREN.

That portion of Trafford Park purchased from the Trafford Estate was developed as Trafford Wharf Road. In this early view, looking eastwards towards Manchester, the canal and main terminal docks lie off the picture to the left, behind the railway wagons. In the distance, the girder arches of the fixed bridge on Trafford Road may be noted. Under construction, centre, is the warehouse for the Manchester & Liverpool Transport Company. Fixed to the railings by the gatepost is a notice which advertises 'DOCK FERRY. STEAMER FROM THE ELEVATOR EVERY FEW MINUTES.' (MSCCo)

This 1901 view shows Trafford Wharf in the opposite direction, and includes the completed building which was but a framework in the previous illustration. By this date, the whole of Trafford Park having been sold in 1896 for development as an industrial estate, new factories were beginning to spring up close to the canal, the advantages of easy access to deep water transport having been stressed as a lure to manufacturers. In the distance, beyond the goods-only swing railway bridge, the outlines of the grain elevator may be seen. The coastal steamer at the wharf is the *'Seagull'* registered in Manchester. (A.E.Bradburn)

Trafford Wharf developed into a very busy location, and was provided with its own coaling stage for locomotives handling the growing traffic. The 1895 swing railway bridge (here seen in the closed to rail/open for navigation position) provided the sole and vital means of linking the rail systems on the two sides of the dock estate, and also allowed access to the many sidings serving the factories of Trafford Park. Connections to the main line railways were made via branches to the London & North Western Railway at Weaste, the Lancashire & Yorkshire Railway at Windsor Bridge, and to the Cheshire Lines via Trafford Park. (MSCCo)

To carry workers from Trafford Wharf around the different parts of the dock estate, and to avoid what would have been a lengthy walk via Trafford Bridge, a small vertical-boilered steam ferry-boat ran every few minutes. Its operator was self-styled *'Captain'* Robert Casey, who would also take visitors on tours of the docks. Here the ferry is departing from the Trafford Wharf landing stage close to the swing railway bridge. (Charles Downs)

In the early years, so many visitors were anxious to see the canal that *'The Ship Canal Passenger Steamer Company'* was established. Paddle steamers ran from Trafford Wharf, offering trips along the whole length of the Canal. For a while the Company flourished, but as the novelty faded, the investment failed. Thereafter, trippers wishing to see the docks were accommodated on the fireboat *'Firefly,'* here giving a demonstration of the power of its water hoses to an all-male visiting party.

MANCHESTER FIRE-BOAT "FIREFLY".

Twenty-three of the 173 steam locomotives employed during the construction period were retained to form the nucleus of the Canal Company's own locomotive stud. Locomotive *'Cadoxton'* (an 1886 product of the Hunslet Engine Company, and named after a location on the Barry Railway on which contractor T.A. Walker had worked) was one which remained, here sporting an outsize headlamp. New locomotives were purchased from 1897 onwards, and were named after ports of the world, a practice which ceased in 1914, after which numbers only were used. The Ship Canal railway became the largest private system in the country. In the 1950s nearly 80 steam engines were in use. (Salford Museums & Heritage Services)

Manchester witnessed the foundation of its own shipping line in 1898 when two second-hand vessels were purchased to work for Manchester Liners. An earlier attempt by Newcastle-based Christopher Furness to establish a service between Manchester and India for the import of raw cotton and the export of finished goods, had been defeated by the opposition of other shippers, but a Canadian subsidy for a North Atlantic service was negotiated on the understanding that Canadian exports of grain and meat would be major cargoes. The line's fifth vessel, the *'Manchester Corporation'* of 1899 emerges from Mode Wheel Locks in the charge of the tug *'Eastham.'*

MODE WHEEL LOCKS SHIP CANAL

TRAFFORD WHARF MANCHESTER SHIP CANAL

Timber was another major import to be discharged on Trafford Wharf. Here a team of dockers unloads planks from the steamer *'Aldersgate'* of London. The cryptic message on the back of this postcard sent by a crew member to his family read : *'Another apology for Manchester-by-the-sea.'*

It was important that ship repair and maintenance facilities were available to ship-owners operating services to Manchester. A group of north-eastern businessmen founded the Manchester Ship Canal Pontoons & Dry Dock Company, and provided floating docks at Ellesmere Port and Trafford Wharf. Here a Greek vessel is cradled in the pontoon on a postcard titled *'In Hospital.'* (T.Pinder)

Three graving docks were excavated on Trafford Wharf, close to Mode Wheel, with the floating pontoon moored in the canal alongside. Lock gates sealed off the dry dock basins from the main canal, and each chamber could be drained once the vessel under repair was properly positioned and supported. Here the 1904 **'Manchester Merchant'** occupies one of the docks. This was the second vessel of this name, the first having been lost in 1903.

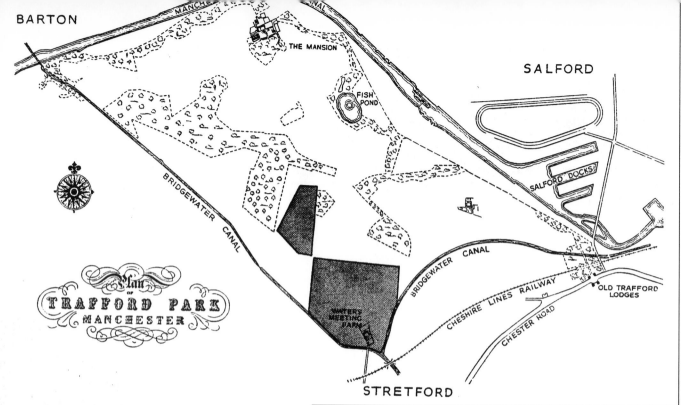

Plan of TRAFFORD PARK MANCHESTER

BARTON

THE MANSION

FISH POND

SALFORD

SALFORD DOCKS

BRIDGEWATER CANAL

BRIDGEWATER CANAL

CHESHIRE LINES RAILWAY

CHESTER ROAD

OLD TRAFFORD LODGES

WATERS MEETING PARK

STRETFORD

Trafford Park was enclosed by the Ship Canal and the Bridgewater Canal, and, apart from members of the de Trafford family and the estate workers, few locals had ever ventured within its bounds. After the arrangement to sell that portion of the estate facing the terminal docks, the family subsequently agreed to dispose of the whole Park. Marshall Stevens, first general Manager of the Ship Canal, moved to become Manager of the Trafford Park Estates Company, charged with the task of developing the Park as an industrial estate. (Trafford Park Estates Co.)

At the time of its purchase in 1896, Trafford Park was predominantly rural, and for some years it remained so. It was expected that industrialists would take land close to the deepwater frontage of the Ship Canal. Trafford Hall was to be developed as a hotel and golf club house. Members of the public were now admitted to the Park's attractions on payment of a small charge '*to keep out the rough element.*' The showground became the venue for annual agricultural shows, visiting circuses, troop reviews, and similar events. (Cooper)

The charge for admission to the Park was abolished as industries began to settle at the eastern end of the estate. Trafford Lake became a popular destination for boating and fishing on summer weekends, and retained its rural character well into the twentieth century, despite the gradual encroachment of the factories. Boats could be hired from William Crook's boat-yard and refreshment rooms.

TRAFFORD PARK LAKE PLEASURE RESORT M/C

Elsewhere in the Park more and more land was occupied by a varied assortment of manufacturing industries, and an extensive network of railway lines flanked the roads and penetrated into the heart of factory premises. Steam engines of the Ship Canal Company hauled wagons between dockside and factory. Boating on the lake ceased as its shores became a waste tip and industrial grime made the area less attractive. The premises of the Carborundum Company advanced to within a few yards of the water's edge. (Imperial)

Of the three main terminal docks for ocean-going ships, number 6 was the shortest with a length of 850 feet. Although the tonnage forecast for the early years was not achieved as rapidly as predicted, the success of the Canal soon became assured. The 'turn-round' time for ships had to be kept to a minimum, and in the early months experienced men were brought in from other ports to oversee local workers in the discharge and loading operations. The use of non-local labour was the cause of the Canal Company's first industrial dispute, when 600 men marched to the docks, threatening to throw *'foreigners'* into the canal. The *'Manchester Miller'* is berthed left, with *'Merganser'* of Cork on the right. (Grosvenor Series)

At the opening of the Canal, No. 8 Dock, 1340 feet long by 250 feet wide, offered the largest expanse for berthing ocean-going ships. In this busy scene, American ship *'Cassie'* of Newport News, Virginia, churns up the water as she leaves her berth. The chevron markings on the funnel of the vessel to the right indicate that it is a ship of the Strick Line, a company which offered regular sailings to Mediterranean and Gulf ports.

Cargoes of fruit quickly assumed a major place amongst the list of imports. Vessels of the Elders & Fyffes line brought regular shipments of bananas from the West Indies to this berth in 8 Dock, where steamships *'Appomattox'* and *'Matina'* (both registered in West Hartlepool) wait to discharge their cargoes. The Elders & Fyffes ships had pale creamy-buff funnels and silver grey hulls, which appeared almost white in sunlight, and were said to be most attractive.

Another north-eastern-based supporter of the Ship Canal was James Knott, whose Prince Line ships quickly established regular services between Manchester and Mediterranean ports, bringing in general cargo, fruit, and Egyptian cotton for the textile industry. Steam escaping from a deck winch partially obscures the name of the *'Spartan Prince'* (built 1897) as she discharges at Salford in 1905. Goods are also being unloaded into waiting barges for onward transmission via connections to narrow-boat canals. This vessel was lost in a collision in 1908. (T.Pinder)

MANCHESTER SHIP CANAL, SALFORD DOCKS. (24)   49781.

The roof of the grain elevator on Trafford Wharf provided a fine location for the early picture postcard photographers. The view eastwards to Trafford Bridge includes the turning basin (centre) and the ends of docks 6-7-8. Many commercial postcards were produced for seamen to inform families of their whereabouts, or to give details of their next voyage, or simply to send a picture of their ship. (Valentine)

From the same vantage point, but looking northwards across the Canal, the Racecourse site awaits development as a further extension of the terminal docks. After the Easter race meeting in 1901, work began on the site to excavate the largest dock, No.9, completed in 1905. In the year 2000, the land is now the site of The Lowry art gallery, theatre and concert hall.

CHAPTER 3

EXPANSION: NUMBER 9 DOCK

'Manchester Races,' first run on Kersal Moor in the seventeenth century, moved to Castle Irwell, Lower Broughton, in 1847, and then, on the expiration of a lease, to the New Barns estate in 1867. Despite the title 'Manchester Racecourse,' all three locations were in Salford. The New Barns land lay to the west of Number 8 Dock, and the possibility that the terminal docks would need to expand on to the Racecourse site had been foreseen even before the full length of the Canal was open. An 1893 arrangement with the Racecourse Company gave the Canal Company the first option to purchase the land if, as was anticipated, it was required for additional docks. Negotiations were complicated by an unwanted intervention from the Trafford Park Estates, and for a time the Racecourse Company contemplated a move to a site in the Park. Eventually, however, it was decided return to the former home, and the Castle Irwell estate was purchased outright. The Canal Company took possession of the New Barns site after the last race meeting in 1901, and work began to excavate what was to become the largest dock of all, 2700 feet long and 250 feet wide. (Race meetings continued on the Castle Irwell site until closure after the November Handicap of 1963. In 1972 portions of the former course were occupied by halls of residence for students at the University of Salford.)

The method of construction for the new dock followed the earlier pattern, work being carried out *'in the dry'* with the excavation sealed off by a substantial earth dam supporting the concrete wall of the main canal. Traffic on the canal was able to continue uninterrupted during the construction. As the excavation neared completion, much of the earth of the dividing dam was removed to leave only the concrete wall to hold back the weight of water.

When ready for filling, a small breach was made in the top of the dam wall, and water was allowed to pour over from the main canal in a steady unhurried flow. A sudden inrush of water might have damaged the construction work, and so a considerable time elapsed before the dock was filled to capacity.

As the dock gradually filled, the piers upon which the wharves were constructed became hidden from view. The height of the quay walls is about eight feet above the water level. Under the surface the piers remain today, normally unseen. In this view looking towards Broadway, the Racecourse Grandstand, left in position for the planned royal opening, is centre right, and the spire of Stowell's Church, a local landmark, may be noted top right. Contractor's equipment litters the area, and the work is far from complete.

When the water levels on each side of the dam equalised, sections of the concrete wall were drilled and filled with explosive charges. The resulting detonations smashed the wall, the debris falling to the bottom, from where it was dredged up or hammered into the bed of the canal. (T.Pinder)

Blasting the old wall for new dock. M.S.C.

The new dock was officially opened by King Edward VII and Queen Alexandra during a royal visit to Manchester on the 13th July 1905. On their way to the dock, the royal procession passed the entrance to Trafford Park, where manufacturers had erected an arch to display their various products. A phrase from a recent speech was quoted above a reminder that 'TRAFFORD PARK IS AWAKE.'

THE ROYAL PAVILION. KING EDWARD & QUEEN ALEXANDRA OPENING
THE MANCHESTER SHIP CANAL NEW DOCK, 13TH JULY 1905.
E.T. & CO.
COPYRIGHT.

On the Broadway side of the new dock a temporary pavilion had been constructed to house the royal party and distinguished guests. Boys from the Lancashire Navy League formed a guard of honour, and it was reported that the king was in good humour and laughed heartily. A bevy of photographers with equipment on tripods stands left. Notice the numbers on the mooring bollards. This postcard was distributed by J.Nall & Company, whose address was given as New Dock Road (an extension of the original Broadway), and who must have been pleased to see their warehouse featured on the royal photograph.

On a given signal, two specially chartered Mersey ferry boats, *'Claughton'* and *'Bidston'*, sailed into the new dock. Shareholders in the Canal Company were allowed to observe the proceedings from the opposite side of the dock as the two vessels sailed past the pavilion and moored by the racecourse grandstand. (T.Pinder)

The celebrations over, the first cargo vessels entered the new dock. Warehouses flanked one side only at this stage. The huge grain elevator which was to dominate the far end of the dock, and additional warehouses on the northern side, were not completed until much later. In the foreground, a drilling and tamping machine is at work on the remains of the old wall. Moored on the right is the second *'Manchester Merchant,'* launched in 1904.

The new dock soon became crowded with shipping of all nations. The postcard photographer once again used the roof of the Trafford Wharf grain elevator to obtain this view across No.9 Dock. Beyond may be seen the smoking chimneys of the tightly-packed terraced houses which once filled so much of this part of Salford. (Grosvenor series)

Number 2 Grain Elevator, at the head of No.9 Dock, was not completed until 1915. Its huge bulk dominated the skyline of the docks. Pipes from the spider-like floating grain elevator, positioned between ship and wharf, are sucking out grain from the ship's hold and transferring it to conveyor belts running beneath the docksides. These belts carried the grain directly into the storage elevator. (Sankey)

Inside the main storage elevators, grain could be weighed, bagged, or transferred in bulk to rail or road transport. Working over the off-sides of ships, the floating elevators could discharge grain direct into barges alongside, for onward transmission via narrow-boat canals to mills elsewhere. The Kellogg Company in Trafford Park had premises on the edge of the Bridgewater Canal and received supplies from the main docks in barges transferred via Hulme Lock.

Timber continued to rank high amongst the leading imports, and the open area of ground on the north-western end of 9 Dock became a vast storage ground. It was this same area which in the late 1960s became the site for Manchester Liners' container base operations. (Sankey)

With the completion of No.9 Dock, the dock estate contained over six-and-a-half miles of quays and hundreds of acres of warehouses, transit sheds, and open storage space. Equipment included over 200 steam-powered or electric cranes, and all the latest appliances designed to give vessels a quick despatch.

Extensive railway sidings were laid on the area of ground between numbers 8 and 9 docks, which became the major marshalling yard for the formation of trains of goods wagons. At the quay opposite, riding high in the water, is moored the *'Manchester Importer,'* built new for Manchester Liners in 1899. In the foreground a vessel of the Prince Line is berthed by the Trafford Wharf grain elevator. The tongue of land in the centre of the picture is now occupied by The Lowry arts centre.

CHAPTER 4 MANCHESTER DOCKS - SALFORD

The completion of the Ship Canal was celebrated as a triumph, but its full potential was not realised as quickly as its promoters had hoped. A variety of cargoes was expected, but it was the cheaper import of raw cotton and the easier export of finished goods which had formed the main argument for the construction of the Canal. Huge quantities of raw cotton did, indeed, come from India and Egypt, and in increasing measures from North America, but, in fact, cotton did not prove the to be the principal import. The opening of the Canal preserved old industries, such as flour milling, paper making, and meat packing, and encouraged new industries to settle along its route. Timber, grain, meat, fruit, and sugar featured strongly amongst the imports, and the bulk carrying of oil was a growing trade which had not been anticipated initially. The outward shipment of locally manufactured goods was facilitated by the Canal, but the tonnage of imports always exceeded that of exports. For exported products, the development of the Trafford Park industrial estate provided a boost to the Canal's fortunes, and made worthwhile the construction of the additional No.9 Dock, though plans for an even larger No.10 Dock were never implemented. In this aerial photograph from the early 1920s, Trafford Wharf extends across the centre of the view, with docks 9, 8, and 7 beyond. In the foreground are the factories of Trafford Park, with rail connections to the dockside. (Canadian Gazette)

Mode Wheel Locks, Manchester Ship Canal.   228.

Having negotiated the 36 miles of the Canal, the mariner's first sight of Trafford Wharf and Salford Docks would be gained as the ship rose in Mode Wheel Locks. As with other locks on the Canal, in order to conserve water the chambers were arranged in pairs, large and small. Sluice gates to the right of the locks controlled the level of the water in the terminal docks. (Commercial postcard)

Manchester Ship Canal.   225.

After rising in the final lock, vessels moved into the last section of the Canal on the approach to the berths. Trafford Wharf is to the right of the picture, with the British Oil & Cake Mills (producers of cattle feed) and the tower of the grain elevator prominent. The large ships moored on the left hide the approach to Salford Quays. (Commercial postcard)

Inward-bound steamship *'West Cobalt,'* pulled by the tug *'Lord Stalbridge'* and guided at the stern by one the Ship Canal's paddle tugs, leaves Mode Wheel Locks on the final stage of the journey up the Canal. To the left are the dry docks, with the General Steam Navigation Company's *'Cormorant'* riding high in the floating pontoon. (Sankey, Barrow)

An aerial view of Mode Wheel Locks and the Dry Docks, show all three graving docks occupied, though the pontoon is empty. The storage tanks at Mode Wheel (top left) were built some time after the Canal opened to cater for the increasing imports of bulk oil. The first imports of oil had been carried in casks. (A.W.Hobart)

An aerial view from above Trafford Wharf shows Salford Quay and the site of The Lowry arts centre as it was in the mid-twentieth century, when the wharfside at that point was used for timber storage. Timber continued to be a major import, and there is evidence of recent cargoes on both Trafford Wharf and on the open ground towards Broadway at the top of the picture. The railway sidings in the foreground hold a train of wagons already loaded with planks. To the right the Canal widens out on the approach to the turning basin. Vessels in the picture include the Ellerman Line's *'City Of Stafford'* (left) and *'Riza Captan'* (foreground). Ship Canal tugs have just swung an unidentified steamer for its return journey to the Mersey. The portion of Trafford Wharf in the foreground is to be the site for the northern branch of the Imperial War Museum. (Airviews)

Another view, dating from about 1922, again taken from the Trafford Wharf side, looks across the turning basin to No.8 Dock. To the right the dredger *'Irwell'* carries out its regular duty of scooping up deposits from the Canal bed, whilst in the centre the busy work-horse of the docks, Captain Casey's ferry-boat, passes a tug as it speeds across in the direction of 9 Dock. (Sankey, Barrow)

Salford Quay, between docks 8 and 9, looking to the Canal in the direction of the dry docks and Mode Wheel. The wharfside at this point was left free of warehouses and other obstacles, and was often used for the loading of heavy lift cargoes. In the peak years of the engineering industry, exports of machinery left from Salford Quay. Steam locomotives from Beyer Peacock, the Vulcan Foundry, or Nasmyth's, were often lined up on rails by the water's edge ready for export overseas.

"BANGOR" C.D.

Timber imports at Salford Quay. A postcard home to Newtowards, Co. Down, from a member of the crew of the steamer *'Bangor'* in 1907 read ; "We sail for Canada on Wednesday night or Thursday morning. If you wish to reply you can address to S.S. *'Bangor'* Salford Docks, Manchester." (Charles Downs)

S/S SLOTHOLM AT MANCHESTER.

Photographer Charles Downs was a regular visitor to the docks, producing postcards at his Trafford Road studio for sale to seamen. His camera captured the timber ship *'Slotholm'* at Salford Quay. It was not unusual for timber ships to carry additional cargo supported by planks propped round the edge of the deck. (Charles Downs)

Until the opening of 9 Dock in 1905, number 8 at 1340 feet long and 250 feet wide was the largest. It remained one of the busiest locations on the docks, and regular shipping services to India and the Pacific coasts of North America berthed here. On the left is the German ship *'Frida Horn'* of Lubeck, whilst the vessel on the right is a 'turret' ship, a design in which the ship's sides turned in to meet the hull above the waterline. (Charles Downs)

No. 6 Dock, here seen crowded with ships waiting for berths, remained the smallest of the docks for ocean-going vessels. Three of the ships are from the fleet of the British & Continental Steamship Company, which operated services to Amsterdam, Rotterdam, Antwerp, Ghent, and Dunkirk. (Charles Downs)

"SAGAMORE" THE CIGAR SHIP.

G. DOWNS.
18. COOKE STREET
OLD TRAFFORD

Unusual visitors to the main docks included the **'Sagamore,'** the *'cigar ship.'* Commissioned by Johnston Brothers, it had been built by William Doxford in 1893 in an experiment to perfect better hull form.

It was the only British example of an American-style 'whaleback.' Problems of classification in Britain, led to its registration in Belgium. It was employed mainly on Black Sea routes, carrying grain. Surprisingly, it had accommodation for 60 passengers. It was sunk by a U-boat in 1917. (Charles Downs)

Amongst the largest vessels to navigate the Ship Canal in the early years were those of the Federal Steam Navigation Company, whose ships bore the names of English counties. Equipped with refrigerated space, the **'Suffolk'** came to Salford first in 1904 with a cargo of frozen meat from Australia and New Zealand. She was 58 feet wide and 500 feet long. Moored at Salford Quay, the masts are telescoped to enable her to pass under the bridges on the Canal. (Charles Downs)

"SUFFOLK".

G. DOWNS.
18. COOKE STREET
OLD TRAFFORD

A twin-funnelled cargo ship was a rarity. Few were built, a second funnel being regarded as an extravagant luxury, rather than a necessity. Frank Strick's *'Tabaristan'* of 1907 may have been the only example of such a ship ever to come to Salford. The second funnel was possibly an attempt to improve boiler room ventilation. The vessel had an interesting career, being sold to the Admiralty in 1913 for conversion to a destroyer depot ship. She was commissioned in 1915 as **H.M.S. *'Diligence'*** and broken up in 1926. (Charles Downs)

"PILAR-DE-LARRINAGA."

The Miguel de Larrinaga Steamship Company, originally a line of sailing vessels under the Spanish flag, established its head office in Liverpool, and in 1896 began a regular service from Galveston to Manchester, bringing in raw cotton. The fleet of some 14 steamers were named after members of the Larrinaga family. The *'Pilar De Larrinaga'* of 1918 was the largest ship in the fleet for some years, trading betwen Salford Docks and ports of the U.S.A. (Charles Downs)

MANCHESTER HERO

Manchester Liners suffered badly during the 1914-18 War. The *'Manchester Commerce'* gained the unenviable distinction of being the first merchant ship to be mined when she was lost off Ireland in 1914. Another ship was requisitioned by the Admiralty, and no fewer than nine others were lost as the war progressed. The Northumberland Shipbuilding Company had a vessel under construction for Austrian Lloyd, which was taken over to become the *'Manchester Hero'* of 1916, seen here with added gun emplacements and camouflage paint. (Charles Downs)

1918.

'CITY OF EXETER' AT MANCHESTER,

The application of camouflage dazzle paint and the obliteration of ships' names were usual precautions during the First World War. The Ellerman Line's *'City Of Exeter'*, here moored at Salford Quays, made two trips to Salford in 1918, bringing in each time 116 officers and 1338 American troops en route to transit camps elsewhere. (Charles Downs)

Ellerman Line ships *'City Of Marseilles'* and *'City Of Calcutta'* made similar voyages. Despite wartime security, the postcard photographer was on hand on each occasion, and many of his prints were posted off promptly to relatives of the soldiers in the United States. One trooper wrote that he was posting his navy suit home. (Charles Downs)

AMERICAN TROOPS AT THE DOCKS.

Losses suffered by Manchester Liners during the 1914-18 War were partially replaced by two new ships, *'Manchester Brigade'* and *'Manchester Division'* launched in 1918. The *'Manchester Division'* on her maiden voyage from her West Hartlepool shipyard, rammed and sank a German submarine in the North Sea. In 1940, twenty-two years later, the *'Manchester Brigade'* was sunk by a U-boat in the Second World War, but the *'Manchester Division,'* seen here under tow by tug *'Cadishead'* as she leaves Mode Wheel Locks, sailed on until 1953. (Charles Downs)

M/cr "DIVISION"

In the years immediately following the 1914-18 War, the Furness shipbuilding yards produced two main designs of ship for owning companies within the Furness Group. The first comprised a class of fourteen smaller vessels to the same basic design, but with minor variations. One such was the Prince Line's *'Lancastrian Prince'* of 1922, a regular visitor to Salford, and here seen unloading raw cotton in 8 Dock.

The Furness shipbuilders' second, and larger, design is typified by Manchester Liners' first post-war vessel, the *'Manchester Regiment'* of 1922, here being led through Mode Wheel Locks. She was one of six similar turbine-powered ships built by the Furness Group for the North Atlantic service. Originally, Manchester Liners had agreed to take three, but trade recession, American competition, and high fuel consumption caused a change of plan. The five other ships were distributed amongst members of the Furness Withy organisation.

The *'London Importer'* was another 1922 product of the Furness yards, to the same design as the *'Manchester Regiment'* and identical in appearance. She was allocated to Furness Withy's North Pacific services, and sailed from Salford to west coast ports of the United States and Canada via the Panama Canal.

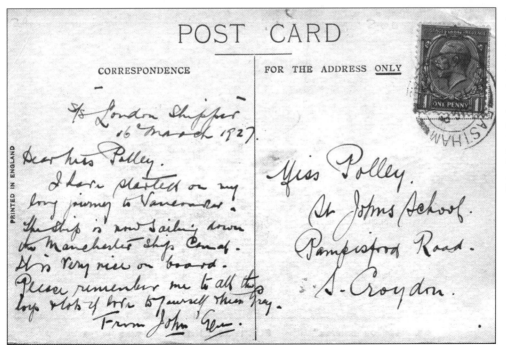

POST CARD

CORRESPONDENCE

FOR THE ADDRESS ONLY

A 1927 postcard from the *'London Shipper'* (1923), another member of the group of six Furness turbine steamers, reads : *"I have started on my long journey to Vancouver. The ship is now sailing down the Manchester Ship Canal. It is very nice on board."* The card was posted at Eastham at the end of the Canal. These ships had accommodation for a limited number of passengers.

For Manchester's Civic Week Procession in 1926, Manchester Liners entered a float advertising their fast freight service to and from Canada and the United States. The cart carried what appeared to be a genuine lifeboat from the then new *'Manchester Commerce.'* The float was photographed on Salford Docks before leaving to join the procession. The hut behind the cart was the Liners' dock office.

During the 1920s, the high fuel consumption of the six Furness turbine steamers had led to the sale or transfer from the North Atlantic run of all but the *'Manchester Regiment.'* By 1930 Furness Withy employed nine newer ships on the North Pacific service, all built between 1924 and 1929 and all having the *'Pacific'* prefix to the name. The *'Pacific Enterprise'* is here outward bound from Mode Wheel, whilst another vessel waits to enter the locks.

THE MANCHESTER SHIP CANAL.

The Canal Company itself operated a fleet of vessels, the most well-known of which were the tug boats. Because restricted speed in the waterway prevented larger ships from attaining sufficient momentum to maintain steering way, the assistance of tugs was often essential. The Company's funnel markings of two white bands were inherited, along with the first tugboats, from the Bridgewater Navigation. *'Barton'* (left) was one of six paddle tugs acquired between 1903 and 1907 for stern towing. Screw tug *'Eastham'* dated from 1899.

The tugboat fleet numbered approximately 30. In 1922 three additional vessels, previously used on a barge-towing service between Ellesmere Port and Liverpool, were acquired from the Shropshire Union Canal Company. The *'Ralph Brocklebank'* dated from 1903, and from 1929 served as the Canal tender for showing visiting dignitaries around the docks. King Fuad of Egypt was on board on this occasion. In 1936 the tug was refitted and re-named 'Daniel Adamson.' (MSCCo)

Beyond the main docks, in order to give the canal a more gentle curve on the approach to Pomona, the original bed of the river was filled in with spoil removed from excavations elsewhere. The fixed bridge on Trafford Road over the former course of the river remained in place, and beneath it was a rail connection to sidings on the Ordsall side. The main bridge has been swung to allow the passage of a tug towing a barge, probably collected from the Bridgewater Canal lock at Hulme. (Commercial postcard)

In the early 1930s a period of great trade depression saw many ships laid up. Although the wharves appear well-occupied in this August 1933 aerial view of 8, 7, and 6 Docks, at least three ships of Manchester Liners remain idle for want of work, and the railway sidings lack their customary crowded appearance.

By the mid-1930s, trade had picked up to such an extent that the docks were busy again, and Manchester Liners began a programme of fleet replacement. This 1935 view of No.8 Dock shows a selection of the tugboat fleet moored amongst the ocean-going ships. The Dock Office, new in 1927, appears at the end of the dock.

NO.8 DOCK. MANCHESTER SHIP CANAL

Moored in 6 Dock in July 1935 were the *'Pandion'* (left) and *'Serula'* (right), two of the twelve vessels of the British & Continental Steamship Company, which operated regular services to Holland, Belgium and France. In the centre of the picture is the *'Manchester Exporter'* (ex- *'Rexmore'*) acquired from the Johnston Line in 1929. The smaller ship alongside the Manchester Liner is the collier *'Kyle Castle.'* (Stewart Bale)

During the 1939-45 War, the docks and Trafford Park came under heavy attack by enemy aircraft. Teams of dockers worked round the clock, despite difficulties caused by the blackout regulations. The dazzle camouflage paint of the 1914-18 war was not revived. Instead, ships were painted a standard battleship grey, and names were obliterated. A floating grain elevator and timber imports dominate this early wartime scene on 9 Dock. The No.1 grain elevator on Trafford Wharf was destroyed in a subsequent air raid.

The huge No.2 elevator at the other end of 9 Dock was impossible to disguise, and was a major landmark for enemy bomb-aimers. German pilots were issued with a book of reconnaissance photographs to enable them to identify targets such as bridges and locks, which, if damaged, would keep the ships in port. Manchester Liners lost three ships as a result of submarine attack, one by collision, and surrendered the old *'Manchester Spinner'* for use as a blockship during the Normandy landings in 1944.

CHAPTER 5 THE OTHER SIDE OF THE ROAD - ORDSALL

When Salford Docks opened for business in January 1894, members of the public judged by appearance to be *'respectable'* were allowed to wander freely. This privilege was soon withdrawn on the advice of the Ship Canal Company's own Dock Police Force, as it was feared intruders might intimidate some of the experienced port workers brought in from elsewhere. Subsequently, high walls enclosed the dock estate, and admission was strictly controlled by police officers posted at the entrances, which were always referred to as 'gates.' On the other side of Trafford Road, in the triangular area of land between the main docks and Pomona, lay the district of Ordsall, filled with tightly-packed streets of terraced houses. Whilst many of the female residents of the area found employment in the cotton mills of Ordsall Lane, the men tended to work either on the docks or in the factories of Trafford Park. Brief glimpses of dock activities might be seen from time to time through the gates, but, security being tight, many of the dock workers' families had little idea of what life was like on the other side of the wall. The wall enclosing the dock estate is seen to the right of Trafford Road in this 1938 view. (E.Gray)

The mills of Ordsall Lane, facing across the Canal to Pomona, lie in the centre of this mid-1930s aerial view. The district of Ordsall, with its concentrated rows of terraced housing, sits between the industrial area and the Trafford Road edge of the dock estate. Trafford Road swing bridge was Salford's only road connection to the factories of Trafford Park. The close proximity of the Ship Canal and the Bridgewater Canal at Throstle Nest (centre right) is apparent. A new lock, constructed at the end of one of the old Pomona Docks in 1994, has replaced the old Hulme Locks further upstream, and now enables small vessels to transfer between the two waterways. (Aerofilms)

The construction of the terminal docks directly influenced a number of the other buildings which sprang up on the other side of the road. One of the first was the original Custom House, sited on Trafford Road at the corner of New Park Road, directly opposite the docks' main gate. As trade increased, the limited accommodation in the Custom House proved inadequate, and it was converted into a Fire Station and Police Office.

The second Custom House was built in the late 1890s only a little further along Trafford Road, facing the dock wall. Between it and the original Custom House (at the end of the row, far left) lay the 'Flying Angel' Missions To Seamen, and the Salisbury Hotel. The latter advertised itself as *'The Finest Residential Hotel in Salford, facing the docks.'* It was owned by Groves & Whitnall's, a famous Salford brewery company. A third Custom House was built within the dock estate in 1970.

A number of Trafford Road tradesmen with premises facing the docks made a speciality of supplying the wants of ships and seamen. At the corner of Hulton Street was a tailor who provided uniforms and cap badges for ships' officers. Amongst the shops in the Salisbury Buildings was that of Harry Fisher, a shipping butcher, whose display would be condemned today as unhygienic.

Catering for seamen in port with money to spend and leisure to spend it, were numerous hotels. The Ship Hotel, at the junction of Trafford Road and Cross Lane, was typical of the larger establishments. It was claimed that at one time Trafford Road and Cross Lane had more public houses per mile than any other road in the land. The hansom cabs on the left stand outside Stowell's Church about 1903.

Catering for spiritual and social needs, were several churches and religious organisations like the Dock Mission, once of Taylorson Street, later of New Park Road. The Dock Mission in particular was a centre for social and leisure pursuits for Ordsall residents. Its helpers provided a free breakfast on Christmas Day for poor children of the neighbourhood. This Mothers' Meeting about 1908 provided a fine display of hats.

Ordsall Park, bounded by Trafford Road, Hulton Street, and New Park Road, provided an oasis of greenery in the midst of the built-up area. Like other Salford parks, it once boasted a lake, complete with swans. Its further, and less picturesque, reaches consisted of cinder or grassless playing pitches for the local school sporting fixtures. (Grosvenor Series)

'Manchester Docks' may have been the official title, but Salfordians were in no doubt as to their true location. After the canal was built, and Trafford Park began to develop as an industrial estate, there was a need to transport masses of workers quickly and cheaply. The area was served first by horse-drawn tramcars, and then between 1901 and 1947 by electric tramcars, which bore the destination 'SALFORD DOCKS' (later abbreviated to 'DOCKS'). Unlike the present Metrolink route, the tramcars did not enter the dock estate, but ran alongside in Trafford Road to Trafford Bridge and Trafford Park. Until the 1920s, the average fare charged per mile was 0.55 pence, the highest fare being threepence. Nearly 70% of the tickets sold were for penny short-distance fares - and the tramways made a profit and contributed to the relief of the rates! The ticket illustrated is for an Ordsall Park-Trafford Park journey. Salford and Manchester exercised joint running powers over the independent Trafford Park lines.

The construction of the new dock offices opened in 1927 provided an opportunity to include a matching entrance arch over the Main Gate on Trafford Road. This later carried the title 'Manchester Docks.' Incorporated into the building was a branch of Williams Deacon's Bank. In a window at the side, a clerk would chalk up on a hinged blackboard details of major arrivals and departures. (J.L.Brown)

Ordsall children were not permitted to enter the dock estate unless on a properly organised official trip. Understandably reluctant to have persons wandering amongst moving cranes and wagons, the Company preferred to convey parties in a motor launch. It was more difficult to arrange a visit to board a ship. For that, one had to wait for a sympathetic captain. Children from St.Cyprian's School surround Captain Brown and officer cadets of the *'Arabian Prince'* on a visit in 1954. Armed with intelligent questions about cargoes, destinations, order of loading, distribution of weight, etc., the main fact remembered afterwards was that the captain had given everyone ice cream. (E.Gray)

When the new Ordsall Secondary School opened in 1957, it was possible from certain rooms to catch tantalising glimpses of life on the other side of the wall. From a window on the top floor, the bow of the *'Arabian Prince,'* a regular visitor to Salford, is seen in Dock 7 alongside one of the floating cranes. Punctually at four minutes to noon each day, entertainment was provided at this location by the driver of a travelling steam crane, who used to pass the window with his bicycle dangling from the crane's jib. (E.Gray)

The long wall and sheds which shut out the docks from Ordsall residents are evident in this 1957 view of Trafford Road. The cream facade of the Dock Office sparkles centre. Extreme left the bulk of the No.2 grain elevator stands out against the skyline. To the right, on the corner of Smith Street, is the side of the second Custom House. (E.Gray)

In their heyday, the docks and the factories of Trafford Park employed thousands of workers. Most were conveyed to and from work twice a day by public transport, and the morning and evening *'rush hours'* on Trafford Road were sights to behold. The time is shortly after 5.00 p.m. on a weekday in the mid-1950s as an unending stream of buses carries the workforce home.(Dennis Gill)

CHAPTER 6
BOOM AND DECLINE, 1950 - 1980

Post-war recovery and the return of manufacturing industry to normal peace-time production saw the start of the busiest-ever period for the Ship Canal. In terms of the amount of tonnage handled, the years 1955-1959 proved to be the peak period since the opening. In four of these years the total reached over 18.5 million tons, as against seven million in the peak year of the 1930s, and less than one million in 1894. Throughout the 1960s and early 1970s, the annual totals ranged between 14 and 17 million tons. In this aerial view of Salford Docks in the early 1950s, vessels crowd No. 9 Dock. Of the buildings in this photograph, only the Dock Office (centre top) remains today. (Airviews)

After the interruption of the war years, the flow of local manufactures exported through Salford Docks resumed. The 60-ton floating crane is here moving along No.8 Dock carrying a railway coach ready for loading on a ship bound for Portugal. Beyond is the Cayzer Irvine Clan Line steamer *'Clan Alpine.'* The Clan Line steamers operated services to East African and Indian ports. (Bert Wilson)

One of the largest and earliest factories in Trafford Park was the Westinghouse, which became Metropolitan Vickers (later Amalgamated Engineering Industries, then General Electric Company). Electrical equipment was exported all over the world. The tug *'Cadishead'* shepherds one of the floating cranes as it lifts a 98 ton transformer.

Imports continued to exceed exports. Some of the dusty or dirty bulk cargoes, particularly carbon black, were unpopular with dockers, and merited higher rates. Here, sulphur is being unloaded by grab crane from the American vessel *'Joseph Lykes'* of Houston, and discharged direct into waiting railway wagons on the quayside.

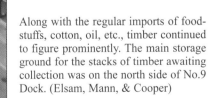

Along with the regular imports of foodstuffs, cotton, oil, etc., timber continued to figure prominently. The main storage ground for the stacks of timber awaiting collection was on the north side of No.9 Dock. (Elsam, Mann, & Cooper)

Many of the exports through Salford Docks originated in factories far from the region. Furness Withy's services between Manchester and the west coast of North America regularly carried exports of motor cars to the West Indies, Panama, and Pacific ports. Rows of Hillman cars wait at the end of 8 Dock to be loaded on the *'Pacific Shipper.'* The vessel, built in 1924, was at that time one of the oldest in the Furness fleet, being withdrawn in 1950.

Much of Manchester Liners' Canadian cargo was trans-shipped at Montreal. Knowing of the Canadian Government's plans for the St. Lawrence Seaway project, the Company developed an early foothold in the direct trade to Great Lakes ports with two small ships of a size suitable to negotiate the existing locks on the canals linking the Lakes. The *'Manchester Pioneer'* was launched at Cammell Lairds's in 1952, shortly followed by the *'Manchester Explorer.'* (E.Gray)

Prince Line's services between Manchester and Mediterranean ports carried general cargo as required. The *'Arabian Prince'* of 1938 was one of the smaller vessels, and called at some unusual ports. She was photographed in 8 Dock in May 1958 in her last full year of service, before being sold for breaking up in 1959. (E.Gray)

The original single-track swing railway bridge of 1895, connecting Trafford Wharf with the rest of the dock estate, proved inadequate for the increased traffic of the Second World War. A double-track replacement was installed on the same spot in 1943, and it is this same bridge, moved to a new location acoss 9 Dock (and renamed *'Detroit Bridge'*), which is now the pedestrian walkway across Erie and Huron basins. The locomotive, number 90, was the last steam engine to be purchased by the Ship Canal Company, and worked between 1954 and 1964. (Elsam, Mann & Cooper)

Because it catered mainly for smaller vessels, in later years the depth of water at Pomona Docks was permitted to be less than elsewhere. By the second half of the twentieth century, masters of vessels berthing at Pomona were advised that the maximum draught would be 16 feet, as against 28 or 26 feet in other parts of the Canal. Nevertheless, the removal of accumulated silt remained a regular duty. The bucket dredger *'Irwell'* was at work near Pomona.

The *'Ulster Mariner'* of the Belfast Steamship Company was a regular visitor to Pomona Docks, carrying general cargo between Manchester and Northern Ireland. Built in 1922 as *'Ayrshire Coast'* of Coast Lines, she had sailed for the Burns & Laird Line before joining the Belfast fleet in 1947. She was 32 years old when photographed at Pomona in August 1954, being scrapped in the following year. (E.Gray)

The Ship Canal proper ended at Pomona. Upstream beyond Pomona, traffic was limited to barges going to or from the old Hulme Locks of the Bridgewater Canal, located to the right under the railway viaduct. These gave access to the narrowboat canal network and the Castlefield area of Manchester. The Woden Street footbridge of 1878 (unofficially known as *'Mark Addy's Bridge'* after that gentleman's life-saving activities on that part of the River Irwell) pre-dated the canal. Motor vessel **'Parfield'** tows barge **'Flaxmore'** beneath the bridge. Commercial use of the Bridgewater Canal continued until 1974. (C.A.Appleton)

In the 1950s the Canal Company purchased a fleet of thirteen small diesel-engined tugs for special duties. Most were attached to the dredging department, and towed barges of silt to deposits elsewhere. Small craft such as these were expected to pass under the swing road bridges, where the clearance was 15 feet or more when closed, but the swing railway bridge at Trafford Wharf had a clearance of only 2 feet 9 inches. **'Deborah,'** new in 1958, pulls a barge beneath Trafford Road in August 1960, as the railway bridge begins to open. (C.A.Appleton)

The Canal Company's fleet of steam locomotives began to be replaced by diesel engines in 1958. The maintenance workshops were sited at Mode Wheel, but smaller locomotive depots could be found at strategic points up and down the Canal, housing and servicing engines where they were most needed. This was the locomotive shed at New Barns, between 8 and 9 Docks. Engine number 50, a Hudswell Clarke product of 1907 (formerly named *'Australia'*) stands outside. It was withdrawn in 1961. (C.A.Appleton)

By 1967 the last of the steam locomotives had been withdrawn. Two were sold for preservation elsewhere, but many were scrapped on the sidings close to Mode Wheel workshops. Locomotive 22 (formerly named *'Rotterdam')* with 53 (*'Sweden'*) behind, were being cut up in April 1966. (E.Gray)

Despite the set-back of the 1966 seamen's strike and occasional labour problems ashore, the docks remained busy. Steamers of the Clan Line were regular visitors to new facilities provided on 6 Dock. *'Clan Macintosh'* was loading for South African ports, whilst *'Clan Maclaren'* was about to depart for Mauritius. (MSCCo)

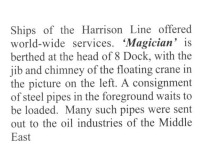

Ships of the Harrison Line offered world-wide services. *'Magician'* is berthed at the head of 8 Dock, with the jib and chimney of the floating crane in the picture on the left. A consignment of steel pipes in the foreground waits to be loaded. Many such pipes were sent out to the oil industries of the Middle East

For a time after 1967 Manchester Liners acted as agents for Irish Shipping Limited. The United States Lines had withdrawn from the Manchester-New York service, and as the amount of cargo from Dublin to New York was often insufficient, the *'Irish Spruce'* and the *'Irish Poplar'* were available to fill the gap. The *'Irish Spruce'* is in 9 Dock loading for Baltimore, New York, and Norfolk, Virginia, in 1970. Tug *'Sabre'* tows out the German ship *'Christiane Schulte'* stern first. The *'Irish Spruce'* was lost by stranding in 1972. (Norman Edwards Associates)

Confidence was high enough at this period for Manchester Liners to move from their former headquarters in St.Ann's Square, Manchester, to the new Manchester Liners House (now Furness House) opened on the dock estate in December 1969. The building was designed to resemble the bridge of a ship, facing towards Manchester town centre. Part of the grain elevator on 9 Dock can be seen to the right of the picture. (Norman Edwards Associates)

In the late 1960s, competition on the North Atlantic routes, coupled with rising shore costs and labour problems, prompted Manchester Liners to place orders for three specially-built container ships, the first to be commissioned by a British shipping company, and to invest in the provision of suitable terminals in Manchester and Montreal. The *'Manchester Courage'* of 1968 worked on this pioneer service from the new container base by the end of 9 Dock.

In 1968 Manchester Liners had taken over the Prince Line's Mediterranean services. The success of the Canadian container traffic encouraged the Company to adopt the same methods to other services, and the older members of the fleet were gradually replaced by container vessels. A smaller ship, the *'Manchester Merit'* of 1970, here being swung in the turning basin, was first employed on feeder services between Montreal and Chicago, but afterwards became the first British container ship to work in the Mediterranean. (John Cooper)

Handling of containers on the quay was done by straddle carrier and transporter crane. The new methods of working were confined to the container terminal. Elsewhere on the docks, ships discharged and loaded as before. This 1971 view of No.9 Dock, looking from the grain elevator end towards the terminal, shows the rest of the quaysides occupied by traditional vessels. In the far distance, under the transporter crane, is one of Manchester Liners large container ships.

Number 8 Dock, viewed from Trafford Wharf in October 1973, looking across the turning basin, has the motor vessels *'Pool Fisher'* of Barrow and *'Hawthorn'* on the left, with a Greek ship right. The top floors of the Manchester Liners House rise above the warehouse roofs. A series of dock strikes in 1971-72 had undermined confidence, and the number of large ships passing all the way along the Canal; began to decline.

The Dry Docks in April 1974 contained the **'Daniel Adamson,'** much altered from its days as the Shropshire Union Canal's **'Ralph Brocklebank,'** but still retaining its steam-driven machinery long after steam-power had vanished from the rest of the tug-boat fleet. The vessel is now preserved at the Ellesmere Port Boat Museum. (Sadly, the paddle tug **'Old Trafford'** has now been removed from display at Greenwich during reorganisation of the National Maritime Museum. The Museum's stewardship of this unique specimen has been scandalously irresponsible, and the future of its surviving portions remains in doubt.)

The old steam lighter **'Basuto'** was a common sight in Salford Docks. Originally a Clyde 'puffer' of 1902, she had later worked on the Mersey for William Cooper, carrying sand and stone. The Dry Docks Company acquired her in 1928, and fitted her with a wheelhouse and a winch (from an old Manchester Liner). **'Basuto'** had a remarkably long, if unglamorous, life on general repair and maintenance duties around the docks. She was still active as late as 1978.

At Pomona roll-on roll-off facilities were made available in No.3 Dock for specially-designed ships to transport heavy loads of up to 300 tons. The *'Starman Africa,'* moored at the bend in the Canal by the entrance to No.4 dock, though capable of using the heavy lift berth, was using her own on-board crane - hence the pronounced list to starboard.

Trafford Wharf in August 1973. The *'Ocean Transport'* of Swansea was unloading grain via the floating elevator for Kellogg's Trafford Park factory. Kellogg's factory was located on the banks of the Bridgewater Canal, and until 1974 grain was conveyed onwards by barges transferring to the smaller waterway at Hulme Locks. (C.A.Appleton)

A crane operator's view of a Manchester Liner. The *'Frontier'* was a small cellular container ship chartered from Spanish owners between 1972 and 1979 for the Mediterranean services. On the quayside is one of the 'straddle carriers' transporting a container for loading by crane. (Norman Edwards Associates)

In 1973 Manchester Liners took delivery of two general purpose vessels, *'Manchester Vigour'* and *'Manchester Zeal,'* which could be used on both Atlantic and Mediterranean services. Both were originally flush-deckers, but experience in service led to a change of opinion as to their suitability, and in 1975-76 both were sent to a German shipyard to have forecastles added, as seen in this 1977 picture of *'Manchester Zeal'* at the container terminal. (Norman Edwards Associates)

Two large 12,577 ton container ships, *'Manchester Reward'* and *'Manchester Renown,'* on order from Smith's Dock, Middlesbrough, arrived in 1974 at a time of trading uncertainty, and were immediately placed out on charter in the Far East, not returning until 1978, when it was decided to operate the North Atlantic service mainly from Liverpool.

A Manchester Liners advertisement for mid-April sailings in 1979 reveals that the two recently-returned vessels are loading at Liverpool, rather than Manchester, and calling at Greenock. The abbreviation FCL meant 'Full Container Load' and indicated point of delivery for loading. LCL stood for 'Less-than-full Container Load.' Part-filled containers could be delivered to Vere Street shed for packing ('stuffing' in dockers' parlance) and forwarding to Liverpool by road. Though her two sister ships (*'Manchester Challenge'* and *'Manchester Courage'*) were sold in 1979, the *'Manchester Concorde'* loading at Manchester, remained in service until 1982.

MANCHESTER LINERS *CONTAINER SERVICES* **TO CANADA AND THE UNITED STATES**

Through bills of lading issued to all Canadian interior points and certain U.S. points.

			Closing	LCL - 1700 hrs	FCL - 1400 hrs
c.s. **MANCHESTER CONCORDE**	....		Voy 141	Wed Apr 11	Thur Apr 12 (1200 PROMPT)
	LOADS AT MANCHESTER				
*c.s. **MANCHESTER REWARD** (Calls Greenock)	....		Voy 43	Wed Apr 18	Thur Apr 20
	LOADS AT LIVERPOOL				
*c.s. **MANCHESTER RENOWN** (Calls Greenock)	....		Voy 47	Wed Apr 25	Fri Apr 27
	LOADS AT LIVERPOOL				* ALSO LOADS LCL AT MANCHESTER

FCL MANCHESTER: No. 1 Berth, 9 Dock, Salford. LIVERPOOL: Royal Seaforth Dock, Seaforth. GREENOCK: Clydeport Container Terminal

LCL MANCHESTER: No. 3 Vere Street Shed, Dock Rd, Salford. LIVERPOOL: No. 1 Packing Shed, Royal Seaforth Dock. GREENOCK: Clyde Container Services Braehead, Renfrew.

CONTAINER GROUPAGE DEPOTS AT LONDON-BIRMINGHAM-LEICESTER-BELFAST-DUBLIN-GLASGOW

Manchester Liners Limited P.O. Box 189 Manchester Liners House, Port of Manchester, Manchester M5 2XA Tel 061 872 4466 Grams 'NAUTICUS' Manchester Telex 667001 London Tel 01 480 7533 Telex 888868 Liverpool Tel 051 236 3272 Glasgow Tel 041 221 9982 6 Telex 779463 Birmingham Tel 021 643 0244 5

'Manchester Concorde' (12,039 tons, left) and 'Manchester Faith' (1421 tons), berthed at the container terminal about 1979. The latter ship, the second to bear that name, was one of several smaller vessels taken on charter in the 1970s as traffic demanded. The difference in size is apparent. (Norman Edwards Associates)

The two cranes at the container base had a lift capacity of 25 and 35 tonnes respectively. Heavier items were occasionally carried, and could be loaded over the off-side of ships by the heavy duty floating crane, here lifting a steam generating unit. (Norman Edwards Associates)

Competition for cargoes on the North Atlantic service eventually led Manchester Liners to co-operate with former rivals in providing a weekly service to Montreal from Felixstowe, calling at Hamburg, Antwerp, and Le Havre as required. The larger ships no longer came to Manchester, but smaller vessels were chartered to continue the Mediterranean services. The *'Manchester Clipper'* was chartered from German owners in 1980-83. (Norman Edwards Associates.)

By 1983 there was very little traffic on the upper reaches of the Ship Canal. Manchester Liners transferred their remaining Manchester services to Ellesmere Port. The *'Manchester Fulmar'*, on charter 1981-83, was amongst the last vessels to trade from the container base on 9 Dock. The Ship Canal Company faced the problem of operating costs far exceeding revenue. (Norman Edwards Associates)

CHAPTER 7 THE SALFORD QUAYS PROJECT & REVITALISATION OF THE OLD DOCKLANDS

By the early 1980s the Ship Canal Company had begun to explore the possibility of new uses for the Salford end of the Ship Canal. Changes in the patterns of trade, competition, and the increase in the size of container ships meant that few vessels now sailed the full length of the Canal. Even Manchester Liners had moved elsewhere, and they were soon to vanish altogether, absorbed into the Orient Overseas Container Line. Thus it was that in 1981 a substantial part of the docklands was declared an Enterprise Zone, and new businesses were attracted to what was once derelict land. A scheme for waterside development around Dock 6 was proposed in 1982, and the full Salford Quays Development Plan was published in 1985, concentrating on the most important environmental aspects of the site - water, roads, and public access and landscape.It was proposed to enclose the docks 7, 8, and 9, and to improve the water quality ; a new road network was to be established ; and there was to be public access to extensive walkways with attractive landscaping. Work began promptly, major portions being completed in 1990. By 1991, the only large site remaining available was that reserved for what was then to be named the *'Salford Centre For The Performing Arts,'* subsequently renamed the Lowry Centre. The commemorative stone records the partnership between the City of Salford and the Department of the Environment at the start of the redevelopment in 1986. The logo, which also appears on street signs in the Quays area, is a representation of the pattern of the terminal docks.

Present-day developments have transformed both the first Salford Quay and its better-known successor further down-stream. The original Salford Quay of the 1740s was opposite Manchester's city centre, between New Bailey Street and Blackfriars bridges. Albert Bridge on New Bailey Street was built in 1844, replacing a narrower toll bridge erected in 1765 at the same spot. The wharves of the old Salford Quay Company lay on the far side of the bridge. The New Bailey Street landing stage for riverboat passengers (left - see page 11) fell into dereliction, but is now the starting point for occasional boat trips since the opening of the *'Mark Addy'* public house. (E.Gray)

The *'Mark Addy'* restaurant, brain-child of entrepreneur Jim Ramsbottom, was built into the arches below road level on the site of the old landing stage, once said to be the busiest spot on the river. Beyond the bridge rises the new riverside development on the site of the original Salford Quay, an area which is now known as 'Chapel Wharf.' (E.Gray)

In 1995 the Calatrava Bridge (named after the Spanish designer) was erected over the Irwell, linking Salford's Quay Street and Chapel Wharf (left) with the Parsonage area of Manchester. Some of the stonework of the original Salford Quay can still be seen just above water level. The new bridge is said to represent the sail of a ship. It is the first bridge to span the Irwell between Manchester and Salford for over 100 years. (E. Gray)

Downstream from the wharves and warehouses of the original quays, Salford Corporation's refuse disposal department constructed a dock opening off the river near Wilburn Street into their 'manure depot' (the MD on the right of the bridge) where 'nightsoil' was loaded into barges and towed away down the old river navigation to be deposited elsewhere. Later filled in and abandoned, in recent years the historic dock has been excavated and restored. The cast-iron bridge over the entrance bears the date 1864 together with the names of the Chairman and Engineer. (E.Gray)

Between Pomona and Trafford Road, a new bridge opened in December 1999 carries the Metrolink rapid transit line across the Ship Canal to Exchange Quay, and then onwards across Trafford Road into Salford Quays. A short distance away (off the picture to the left), the 1893 Trafford Road swing bridge remains in use, but is now fixed in position and cannot turn. It carries one-way northbound road traffic only. Alongside the old swing bridge is a new construction carrying traffic in the opposite direction. (E.Gray)

Downstream from Regent Bridge and the old Hulme Lock, the Pomona docks are also undergoing redevelopment. Looking towards the Manchester city skyline from the platform of the new Pomona tramway station, the openings of the old docks may be seen right. A new office building off to the right is named Daniel Adamson House. (E.Gray)

Passing through the present-day Salford Quays, the new tramway passes across the end of Ontario Basin (the old No.8 Dock), where two cranes have been preserved to remind visitors of the area's history. Behind the cranes are two surviving buildings from an earlier period, the 1970 Custom House (left) and the 1969 Manchester Liners House, now Furness House. (E.Gray)

Names allotted to the new basins and other areas of the Quays have been chosen to reflect the former trading connections, particularly commemorating Manchester Liners' services to the Canadian Great Lakes region. The quaysides have been planted with maple trees, and there is an extensive network of footpaths around the former docklands. (E.Gray)

The old No.8 Dock, Ontario Basin, was formerly open to the large area of water titled 'The Harbour' on current plans, but which was really the old turning basin. The dock has now been sealed off, and access is via a small lock, crossed by this Dutch-style lifting bridge. Three of the four main terminal docks have been sealed from the canal proper, but Dock 6, now 'South Bay,' has been left open to the canal for a marina. (E.Gray)

Ontario Basin is now the venue for assorted activities and attractions, including model yacht racing. An aeration system to improve and maintain water quality has been successful and the water is now pure enough to permit water sports. The sealed basins have been stocked with fish, and fishermen are now a common sight on the quaysides. The vessel is the replica of Drake's ship *'The Golden Hinde'* which was on a promotional visit. (E.Gray)

Two new canals, Mariners Canal and Chandlers Canal, have been cut to permit navigation between the three sealed basins. The entrance to Mariners Canal, leading to Erie Basin, the former No.9 Dock, is seen here with the Victoria office building at Harbour City beyond. On both sides of the new canal are areas of private housing development. (E.Gray)

The old double-track swing railway bridge, erected in 1943 to link Trafford Wharf and the rest of the dock estate, was successfully removed and floated from its original position, and is now a pedestrian bridge between the Erie and Huron Basins, the two halves of the old No.9 Dock. Its new title is Detroit Bridge. (E.Gray)

In August 1998 Salford Quays was the venue for the National Waterways Festival. Hundreds of narrow boats arrived from all parts of the British Isles, and No.9 Dock (Huron Basin, viewed from the pedestrian bridge) was once again crowded with vessels, but of a type not previously seen in Salford Docks. On the extreme left construction of The Lowry centre has begun. (E.Gray)

The Royal Navy was represented at the 1998 Waterways Festival in the shape of P270 H.M.S. *'Biter'* here seen moored in Ontario Basin. In the background the Holiday Inn was at that date under construction, a most regrettable planning decision, since its solid bulk overshadows the picturesque lock and spoils the open access view towards the expanse of the turning basin. (E.Gray)

The transformation of Salford Quays and Trafford Wharf consists, in the main, of new high quality commercial, residential, and leisure developments, with numerous restaurants, hotels, cinemas, and now the Lowry art gallery and theatre complex. But on Trafford Wharf at the Dry Docks, occupied by Lengthline Limited, ship repairing proceeds much as before. In February 2000 the *'Briarthorn'* of Liverpool was in one dock, the *'Solway Fisher'* of Dundalk had just entered another, and three more vessels were moored in the canal awaiting attention. (.E.Gray)

Beside some of the new offices on Trafford Wharf are several circular fencing panels which, when viewed directly from the front appear to have straight bars, but which seen from an angle, show the silhouettes of various ships. Two are seen here against the backdrop of an office building. Amongst the series of clever designs is one which is unmistakably a Manchester Ship Canal tugboat. (E.Gray)

Close to the site reserved for the northern branch of the Imperial War Museum is moored H.M.S. *'Bronington'* the last of the Royal Navy's conventional wooden-hulled minesweepers. It was at one time commanded by Prince Charles. Withdrawn in 1988, and now owned by the Bronington Trust, it is maintained as a permanent tourist attraction. Attempts to have the royal yacht *'Britannia'* moored alongside sadly came to naught. (E.Gray)

Samuel Platt was an Oldham industrialist and director of the Manchester Ship Canal Company. It was his yacht, the *'Norseman,'* which led the procession of ships on the opening day in 1894. He might have been amused to know that a century later he would have a restaurant and public house on Trafford Wharf named after him. From a viewpoint near the restaurant in 1999, the Lowry Centre could been seen rising on the sky line. It was by the *'Samuel Platt'* that the swing railway bridge crossed the canal, and the restaurant designer made use of one of its suuports for a small extension. The other piers on which the bridge once turned still remain. (E.Gray)

From the Trafford Wharf side of the turning basin, the silver panels of the Lowry Centre glisten in the sunlight. The dry docks are situated on the left downstream, beyond H.M.S. *'Bronington,'* so vessels heading for the repair facilities do not need to pass beneath the bridge. Few other large ships now rarely venture this far up the canal, so a lifting pedestrian bridge may be considered something of an extravagance. It does rise on occasions to permit the passage of vessels. It is here seen in the lifted position in February 2000. (E.Gray)

Map of Salford Quays. (Alan Palmer)

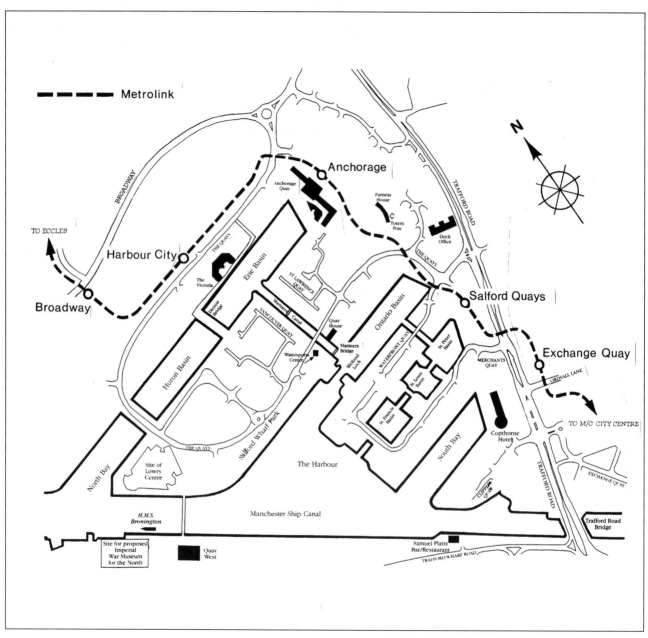

ACKNOWLEDGEMENTS

The original idea for this publication came from Cliff Hayes, who is very good at thinking-up things to keep this writer occupied in retirement. Once the project was under way, a number of people were approached for help, advice, information, or permission to use illustrations, and, as always, all readily and cheerfully gave their support. A book of this nature relies heavily on the reproduction of photographs taken by others. The writer's collection of old postcards and assorted photographs was begun over 50 years ago, when items could be picked up for a few pence. The writer's own photographic excursions did not begin until 1954. A succession of Ship Canal Company public relations officers over the years kindly tolerated an outsider's interest, provided prints, and issued photographic permits to visit the docks. The support of current officers of the Manchester Ship Canal Company, Robert Hough and Alan Dickinson, has been greatly appreciated, as also has the permission to reproduce photographs from the Company's archives. In this respect, the writer acknowledges the prompt assistance of Gabriel Drew, of the Greater Manchester County Record Office (GMCRO), custodian of the Ship Canal photographic records, and of Diane Lee, Ken Craven, and Christine Ellis of the former Salford Quays Heritage Centre, now sadly closed. The staff of Salford Local History Library answered queries and produced maps with their customary efficiency, and the directors of Lengthline Limited generously allowed the writer access to the dry docks. Captain Eric Askew, formerly of Manchester Liners, provided the answers to several queries. The writer also acknowledges the help offered by John and Sara Cooper (formerly of Norman Edwards Associates, publicity agents for Manchester Liners), Ken Hore, Reg Wilson, and the late Alex Appleton. Alan Palmer once again produced a map in his usual excellent manner. Illustrations are acknowledged individually where the source is known, and apologies are offered for any inadvertent omissions. Extensive use has been made of the commercial picture postcards published by ship photographer the late Charles Downs, who produced a unique record of life on Salford Docks.

Published sources of information include the invaluable 'History Of The Manchester Ship Canal' by Bosdin Leech ; R.B. Stoker's 'History Of Manchester Liners' ; John Corbridges's 'Mersey & Irwell Navigation' ; miscellaneous articles in the 'Port Of Manchester Review' ; assorted documents issued by the Company ; and publicity material from the Salford Quays Project Office and the Lowry Centre.

Once again the writer records his sincere thanks to his wife Kathleen, without whom nothing would be produced, who provides the right working atmosphere, urges caution when it is necessary, and who is a fount of useful advice when a second opinion is needed on whether to use this picture or that, or say one thing or the other.

Ted Gray.

Salford 2000

Author's Details

Edward Gray, more usually known as Ted, has held a lifelong interest in local transport history, particularly in the Salford tramway system and the ships of the Manchester Ship Canal. Educated at the old Salford Grammar School in Leaf Square, he was subsequently a student at Westminster College, and has a degree in economic history from the University of London. He began his teaching career in the Ordsall area of Salford, which was very convenient for keeping an eye on activities in the docks. His wife Kathleen was also a teacher, and they met in 1957 whilst serving on the staff of the then new, now recently demolished, Ordsall Secondary School. His subsequent career took him to Lancashire, Oldham, and Manchester, where he was Senior Lecturer in Education at Didsbury Teacher Training College. In 1970 he was appointed Head Teacher of Walkden High School, Worsley, where he remained until retirement. Since leaving teaching, he has been the author of a number of articles and books on transport history.

Other books by available Edward Gray
Greetings from Old Salford
Greeting from Old Eccles
Manchester Liners
A Century of the Manchester Ship Canal
Manchester Trams and Buses

Old HAMILTON

by

Rhona Wilson

This car was photographed in Hamilton in 1901. Licence plates didn't appear until a couple of years later.

C000244859

© Stenlake Publishing Ltd. 1996
First Published in the United Kingdom, 1996
by Stenlake Publishing Ltd.
Telephone: 01290 551122

ISBN 1 872074 83 9

The Avon Mill (on the left of this picture) survived for over three centuries, only to be destroyed by fire in 1963. Originally the property of the Dukes of Hamilton, it was gifted to the town in 1725. This picture was taken from the Telford Bridge, authorised by parliament in the early decades of the nineteenth century to improve the Glasgow to Carlisle turnpike route. Legend has it that the old Avon Bridge – the first bridge beyond the mill – was built on the whim of a rich priest. Wanting to vote on a matter in town, he lost his chance because the river was too swollen to cross. After much expenditure the situation was rectified and our priest, with his own special crossing point, was secure of casting his vote for ever more. Some years ago the bridge prevented the building of a hotel nearby because no-one could work out exactly who owned it.

Introduction

Hamilton was originally called Cadzow (meaning 'beautiful castle') and was used as a summer retreat by King Rederech of Strathclyde in the sixth century. One wag touted the Ha' Mill of Sheilinghill as the source of the district's new name, but this of course is nonsense, and documentation dating back to the mid-fifteenth century records that it was actually changed in honour of its feudal lords, the mighty Hamiltons. They acquired the Barony from Robert the Bruce when he won the Battle of Bannockburn, and after that the old name of Cadzow fell into disuse.

The seat remained in the Hamilton family with only one or two gaps, signifying political disputes with the crown. It was not uncommon for landed gentry to fall out of favour with the monarchy. Duchess Anne, for example, was sympathetic towards the Covenanters, while the eighteenth century Hamiltons were less than enamoured with the 1707 Act of Union, although they chose not to get involved in the violent protests erupting at the time.

By the end of the eighteenth century Hamilton still had an agricultural-based economy, supporting a comparatively large population of 5,000 on crops such as oats, pease, beans and barley. The district was widely used as pasture, with around 2,000 sheep being brought in each year for fattening. As new farming practices were introduced, most of its lands were enclosed with hedges and fencing, allowing greater control over livestock and crops. The arrival of the humble potato was credited with ending the spectre of famine, and many families rented strips of land to grow this staple foodstuff on.

Weaving and lace-making subsequently became the main industrial players in Hamilton. At the turn of the eighteenth century 450 local looms were employed by the Glasgow manufacturers to spin linen and cotton yarn. Forty years later there were well over 1,000 looms with the weavers specialising in cambric weaving. As well as increasing Hamilton's population – which doubled to 6,500 in a fifty year period from the middle of the eighteenth century – the weavers had a part in shaping the town, since streets of houses had to be built to accommodate them. Lace-making was introduced to the district on a whim of one of the Duchesses who decided that she fancied some and, in *enfant terrible* fashion, set up a cottage industry to provide it.

In the 1820s, the weaving industry went into a dramatic decline in Hamilton and elsewhere when the end of the Napoleonic wars resulted in a dearth of orders for blankets and uniforms. Twenty years later the town's weavers were reduced to marching the streets with what they considered to be an underpriced web of cloth; a desperate and impotent protest. Just as well, then, that the 1850s saw the discovery of rich coal seams to provide alternative employment. By 1878 there were around forty working pits, with most of the swollen population earning a living at them. In the following fifty years Hamilton's population increased threefold to over 39,000.

This burgeoning population required an infrastructure to support it. In the early 1830s Hamilton Gas Works was erected by public subscription in Woodside Walk. A few years later there was an attempt to bring in the Police Burgh Act which would have given an elected council the right to raise taxes for various services; in particular to improve the parched water supply. Hamiltonians weren't impressed by the projected rates, however, and the move was thrown out leaving provision of utilities at the mercy of public funds once again. The blossoming coal industry generated both passengers and cargo, and railways arrived in the district to supplement the existing road and bridge network.

Hamilton received blow after blow in the 1920s. Its mining industry collapsed as the pits were worked out, and the Duke of Hamilton sacrificed his palace to eke out the last few scuttle-fulls of local coal. The town's self-esteem sunk in tandem with the palace, and the departure of the Dukes and vacation of the barracks didn't help matters. Hamilton has subsequently had mixed fortunes. By the 1950s its main industry had mutated again, as the town became an administrative centre for the surrounding county. Three decades later there was 20% unemployment, but the development of Strathclyde Park had began, along with the restoration of Chatelherault, the Duke's ancient hunting lodge.

Once renowned for its heavy industry, Hamilton has latterly got used to being known as Lanarkshire's shopping centre, and the town is soon to be subject to yet another sheltered shopping development. This will supposedly encroach on lands belonging to Strathclyde Park, and it remains to be seen whether or not it will be to the advantage of either the local environment or the economy.

Rhona Wilson, October 1996

Barncluith Gardens (derived from Baron's Cleugh) were truly ancient, dating back to the late sixteenth century. The estate to which they belonged, with its mansion house and tower, was originally owned by the Machan family and passed into the Hamilton's hands through marriage. Its terraced gardens were the main attraction, although they were being labelled unfashionable by writers as early as the 1790s. A pavilion in the centre of the five walkways provided a resting area and was decorated with eccentric objects such as a dolphin's skull. The estate changed hands a few years ago with the new owner planning to restore the terraces and open a visitor and garden centre. Sadly, as with many a great plan, it didn't happen and the former gardens remain a tangled and overgrown mess on the banks of the Avon.

By the late 1870s there were around forty pits in or around Hamilton, including Earnock, Greenfield and Barncluith (above). Most of the town's inhabitants earned a living working down the mines until the slump of the mid-twenties, quickly followed by the devastation of the late forties when most of the coal was worked out. The colliery building is visible towards the back of this picture, with its coal wagons to the left. Before 1900 all wagons had to display a name plate for the same purpose as licence plates on cars; this particular one was owned by Archibald Russell.

A gymnastic tableau demonstrated outside Hamilton Barracks, *c.*1910.

Hamilton's barracks date back to the late eighteenth century, and were principally used to house the cavalry until the new Maryhill Barracks opened in Glasgow in 1877. Many regiments used the barracks over the years, including the Cameronians, but by the late sixties they were in a dreadful state of disrepair and were demolished. Bell College now marks the site where they once stood.

A plaque appears on the left hand side of Cadzow Bridge commemorating the Battle of Hieton, fought in 1650. One December day Hamilton Covenanters attacked a Cromwell garrison in the early hours of the morning. They managed to capture General Lambert, a famous Roundhead leader, who later escaped to wreak revenge – hence the battle. All the buildings that can be seen to the left of the bridge have now been removed, giving a clear view of the Mausoleum.

8

Cadzow Bridge was built in 1835 along with the road it carries. The town library dominates this picture. Writing in the 1840s, the author of the Second Statistical Account sniped that service at the then library had severely deteriorated since its management was chosen by popular election. At the time local government was still rather primitive, with Hamilton being run by the provost, a handful of minions and seven councillors – pretty tight for a town of its size.

Cadzow Bridge was instigated by an Act of Parliament in 1819. It was paid for by the Duke of Hamilton in a bid to please the council, unhappy about palace schemes to build within the Old Town area. The bridge was widened in 1901, this time with the Tramways Company bearing the brunt of the cost, since it was to allow space for their tramcars. These ran down Cadzow Street for thirty years. The first building on the right now houses Remnant Kings on the ground floor, with Dickson's cameras just along from it. Most of the other tenements are still standing.

A motor-bus heads down Cazdow Street in this 1930s picture. Lanarkshire tramways were allowed to operate omnibus services within a five mile radius of tram routes from 1908, initially as a feeder service. By the twenties this privilege had been extended to cover the whole of the county, and from 1929 the tramway company had dropped its original form of transport altogether, running buses instead. Many small bus companies sprung up around this time. Companies in the vicinity included William Baxter of Blantyre (with his 'Blue Birds') and J.W. & R. Torrance, who operated from a base in Burnbank Road. The latter eventually merged with the Glasgow Omnibus Company of Bothwell Road, and Stewart and MacDonald Ltd, to form Central SMT.

Old Cross, Hamilton.

Townhead Street was formerly the hotspot for entertainment in Hamilton. Feeing fairs were held near where the Odeon now stands, and there were many visits by big name circuses around the turn of the century. The Hamilton Hippodrome opened the doors of its wooden building to the theatre-going public in 1907, managed by local character Rene Clayton. It had a battle on its hands when the cinemas took off and held 'talkie voice' contests in the late twenties using a 'genuine microphone'. Hamilton's first cinema, known by all as the flea pit, was opened by the town bailie in Church Street *c.*1912. It was soon joined by others including the Picture House, La Scala and the Roxy. The first talkie was Showboat which appeared in 1929. Many of the cinemas are now bingo halls, although their rival, the Hippodrome, burned down *c.*1945.

THE OLD CROSS, CADZOW STREET, HAMILTON.

Given the distinction of being Hamilton's Old Cross, this area isn't so very ancient at all. The real Old Cross was actually at the Tolbooth where High Street ran in front of the palace and joined Castle Street and Muir Wynd.

Looking down from Almada Street, the most prominent building on Beckford Street is Adam's Sheriff Court. The building was quite simple at first and began to take shape around the 1880s. Everything on the left hand side of the street has gone, to be replaced by yet more civic offices, this time for South Lanarkshire Council. The furthest building on the right has been replaced by a car park and prefabs containing the most dreaded offices of all, those for the council tax.

Above: Almada Street originally skirted the barracks and was named to commemorate both Wellington's victory in the Peninsular War and Hamilton's status as a military centre. In the late eighteenth century, as the hand-loom industry took off, it filled up with weavers' cottages. Almost all of the buildings above (which replaced the earlier cottages) have now gone, asides from the Sheriff Court (just visible in background on the right) which acts as a useful landmark. The street is now filled with a mis-match of modern facilities including the Almada Tower (opposite the Sheriff Court) and the Water Palace on the left. All the tenements to the right have been demolished, and the grounds of Bell College occupy the site.

Right: Hamilton's County Buildings were opened in 1964. After World War II the district developed as an administrative centre for Lanarkshire, and by the end of the decade large numbers of people were employed there in an admin capacity. Supposedly based on the Empire State Building (its bottom few floors?) the County Buildings look big and space-age for the 1960s but not particularly clever for the 1990s – the concrete is beginning to chip off!

Peacock Cross, just down from Almada Street, was created some time after 1840 and named after the Peacock family, who had a croft at the junction of Burnbank Road and Brandon Street. The spectacular Cross building is intact, although the front entrance has been bricked over and emblazoned with 'Harvey's Bar', the name of its most recent reincarnation. Burnbank Road leads to the right, with Wellhall Road on the other side of the gushet.

The Peacock Cross Cafe is now the site of Equi's Restaurant and Ice-cream Parlour. Peter Equi arrived in Hamilton in 1922 as a green twenty-two year old, initially setting up his business across the road where the Sunline shop now stands. This site was acquired some thirty years later and the Equis ran both for a time, one specialising in ice-cream and the other a restaurant, with customers having to nip across the road if they fancied both! Previously the cafe was called Tony's and was a popular hangout with forties and fifties guys and dolls. Equi's is still going strong and is now run by the third generation of the family. Incidentally, just down from the restaurant is a white-washed cottage which was once home to Blantyre missionary David Livingstone.

This section of Almada Street has changed tremendously. The large tenement buildings on the right have been replaced by a National Garage, with the new funeral parlour standing along from it just where the horse and carriage is. On the left, the large building has been supplanted by a new property accommodating the Silver Tassie tavern and a Chinese takeaway. The roads themselves have been extensively upgraded, with a raised divider section now in place between the two tram-poles and a small roundabout further down the street. All crossing points at the intersection of roads are guarded by disciplinary railings, painted the gorgeous regulation blue that prevails throughout Lanarkshire.

Valentines Series

The area in this turn of the century picture is now covered by Grammar School Square and Portwell Street. Even in the late eighteenth century it was difficult for historians to determine the Old Town's age, although there was a house standing there inscribed with the date 1533. The Old Tolbooth, which dated from the 1640s and was situated in Castle Street, is visible in the background of this picture. It was damaged by subsidence due to the inevitable coal workings, and was demolished in the 1950s. When the Hamilton family left the area in 1922, the Duke donated some of his properties in the Old Town which were used as a kick-start to the council's housing scheme. At the time there was a chronic housing shortage in Hamilton, as in many areas, with the subsequent health and social problems that overcrowding led to.

BRANDON STREET AND NEW CROSS, HAMILTON.

Hamilton's old Town Hall, made redundant by a new building in Lower Auchingramont Road in the late 1920s, has now been demolished and replaced by that most necessary of facilities, a shopping centre. Today, Bairds graces its former site, with Marks and Spencers and a pedestrian bridge (complete with bright and bold mural) a little further along Duke Street. The town centre post office is still in the same Brandon Street site, with the pavement along from it now widened and fenced off. The building to the left of the post office in this picture has been replaced by a branch of the Halifax

Hamilton's first post office was in Church Street. This 1907 picture shows the Postmaster and his staff.

Dewars, pictured here around 1912, was and still is Burnbank's licensed grocer. In 1966 the shop was bought by Murray Hetherington, who owned it for over twenty years. The previous owner had it for just six months. Mr Hetherington sold the shop in 1989 although the new owners haven't bothered to take down his name in the entrance. The tenements across the road from the shop have been demolished to make way for a housing scheme.

Glasgow Road looking towards town. Gilmour Memorial Church, on the left, is still standing as is the tenement block opposite it. The buildings in the background on the right have been demolished and replaced with a block of shops and a medical centre. A development of flats has its entrance around the area where the factor's office was.

Obviously the tram service wasn't *too* frequent when this picture was taken, judging by the loiterers in the middle of the road. Trams arrived in the district during July 1903 when the Blantyre to Wishaw via Hamilton and Motherwell line was opened. This was a phenomenal occasion and an estimated 30,000 punters turned out to spectate or have a go on the first day. Tram routes were extended to peripheral towns throughout the early years of the twentieth century until the First World War put a halt to development. They never really recovered from this setback and the 1920s saw increasing competition from private bus services. Routes were eventually withdrawn throughout the thirties, although the Glasgow tram service survived until the early 1960s.

Glasgow Road, Burnbank

This tenement block on the left hand side of Glasgow Road, Burnbank, has been swept away and replaced by a modern housing scheme and scattered grass verges. The area to the left foreground was formerly the site of Burnbank Station's railway bridge, now marked by a bus-stop roughly opposite Stewart Street. Trains came to the Burnbank area through the machinations of ironmasters such as William Dixon, keen to exploit the coalfields between Bothwell and Hamilton for use in their Coatbridge ironworks. Burnbank was a stop along the Shettleston to Hamilton cargo and passenger route, which opened in 1878. In the 1880s, nearby Udston Colliery was the scene of a tragic mining disaster when over seventy men died in a fire-damp explosion. Hot on the heels of the Blantyre disaster which claimed hundreds of lives, the Udston explosion must have brought renewed insecurity to Hamilton's miners.

The Cross, Burnbank

Burnbank Cross was obliterated with the development of housing schemes in the vicinity. These led to road realignment, and the Clydesdale Bank's strange circular building now marks the approximate spot of the fountain at the cross. The tenement block on the right is the Co-op's new home, while the crow-steps of the district library (originally the police station) are visible a little further down the road. The tram in the picture is heading in the direction of Burnbank roundabout – a huge carbuncle which makes the approach to the district almost impossible for pedestrians.

Burnbank Cross in all its glory, photographed during the 1920s. Everything in this shot has gone to make way for a concrete housing scheme, complete with concrete recreation area near the Clydesdale Bank. High Blantyre Road forks to the right with Glasgow Road on the left.

Udston and Glenlee mansion houses were bought by Hamilton Town Council some time after 1879 for use as fever hospitals. The first record of a hospital in the town goes back to the fifteenth century when the Collegiate Church allocated lands down by the Clyde (and a safe distance from the town) for this purpose. Hamilton suffered its fair share of epidemics throughout the centuries, with smallpox, cholera and typhoid amongst them. Seventy-five children died of the pox in late 1786 and dysentery was mentioned as a new disease sweeping the barracks around the 1820s. There was also a special cholera burial ground in the kirkyard in the 1860s. Udston became one of the main areas to be developed for housing after 1930, although the mansion house hospital is still standing and in use today.

Reid Street still houses Glenlee Primary School. However, the present building is a modern low-level affair, built on the site of the original building (above) roughly thirty years ago.

Burnbank Co-Operative Society

Burnbank Co-operative buildings still stand on the corner of Glasgow Road and Wilson Street, although the Co-op has now moved a short distance away. The earliest section of the building, currently home to Ladbroke bookies, was built in 1896 according to the date on the chimney on the far left. The wing to the right of the picture is dated 1900 and has since been developed as flats, with the entrance underneath the dormer window enlarged to allow access to courtyard parking. Since this picture was taken the corner section has been reclad and reborn as the Udston Social and Recreation Club. A mish-mash of dual carriageways and housing developments, it's arguable whether the town council's radical redevelopment has actually 'Let Burnbank Flourish'.

The entrance to Chatelherault Country Park stands in the village of Ferniegar, once one of Hamilton's mining villages. Henri II of France made the Hamiltons Dukes of Chatelherault in the mid-sixteenth century, and they gave the name to a hunting lodge, linked to the palace by an avenue of trees, that they later built. Documented by various historians as being a copy of Chatelherault Castle, the lodge evidently looks nothing like its French namesake. Locals, intimidated by its French pronunciation, have coined it a near as dammit 'Shattley Row'. During the 1950s the lodge was affected by subsidence and used to house estate workers who weren't supposed to notice such things. However, by the late 1970s it was a roofless ruin. Fortunately, Chatelherault became the focus for a conservation project, with the original quarry used for its stone reopened to rebuild it. The miner's rows in this picture have long since been demolished.

31

It is thought that Hamilton Palace was originally a square tower house, with parts of the building dating back to *c.*1591. The palace grounds, known as the Hieton, occupied the approximate area of Muir Street, Castle Street and the Ice Rink, and provided the Ducal family with the protection of town residents if necessary. Duchess Anne and Duke William made the first extensive improvements to the palace in the 1680s as the Wild West of Scotland calmed down and their finances blossomed. However, these changes, which left the palace's north front intact, were reasonably modest compared to those carried out by Duke Alexander (aka '*Il Magnifico*') throughout the nineteenth century. Under his command the front became the back, two additional wings were built and the exterior was festooned with Corinthian pillars.

Building began on Hamilton Mausoleum around 1844 at the instigation of *Magnifico*, who wanted a suitable resting place for his ancestors. However, he was dead by the time it was finished ten years later, enshrined in an Egyptian princess's sarcophagus he'd bought especially for the occasion. Perhaps Chopin summed up things most accurately after giving the Duke a recital in the 1840s, writing that 'Everyone here seems to me to have a screw loose.' *Magnifico* was heavily involved in the Mausoleum's design, not always to its advantage. One of the lions is 'sleeping', to signify the dead Dukes, and the other 'awake' and meant to guard them. The mausoleum's original bronze doors led to its downfall as a chapel. They helped create a thirty second echo, meaning sermons could not be read out, and the building was used as an expensive ancestral warehouse alone.

The colourful figure of *Il Magnifico*.

33

Magnifico was the main drive behind the adornment of Hamilton Palace. He married the daughter of William Beckford, a prolific collector, and quickly set about following his father-in-law's example. The palace rooms, such as the morning room, above, photographed by Lafayette (a Lord Snowdon of his day), were filled to the brim with various *objets d'art* including Poussin's, Rubens' and Van Dyck's. *Magnifico* must have turned in his grave when the family auctioned off a fair portion of the collection a few decades after his death in the 1880s. The Hamiltons still used the palace from then on, although less frequently. By 1914 the area round about, mined by royalty-paying collieries, was undergoing severe subsidence and the Ducal family evacuated themselves to Dungavel near Strathaven, leaving their six-century old residence to be demolished.

The Hamilton's final house sale took place around the late 1920s, and was a flamboyant affair with many precious items going for a song. One lucky buyer managed to acquire the main hall chandelier for a few quid, and a school in the district got hold of some huge iron railings from the grounds, although they succeeded in installing them upside down. This sofa and its accompanying chairs were acquired by the Verecchia family who owned the Asiago Cafe of Bannatyne Street in Lanark. With their English gilding, silk brocade upholstery and aristocratic pedigree, the Verecchias thought they would do nicely for their ice-cream customers. In later years, they decided the cafe chaise longues looked a bit tatty and cowped them. A Christie's auctioneer shown a postcard of just one sofa, years later, valued it at a mammoth £80,000 to the everlasting mortification of the family who binned it.

Hamilton Salvation Army Band in front of the infamous bronze doors of the Mausoleum, 1922. The bandmaster, Tom Craig, appears in the front row just left of the drums. In the twenties the Mausoleum, like much Ducal property, began to sink due to subsidence, and after slipping down a massive eighteen feet the preserved Dukes were removed to Bent Cemetery. There are conflicting accounts about what happened to the bodies. One writer states that there were plans to return Alexander and co. to the Mausoleum in the 1970s, with the Hunterian Museum using special techniques to locate family members in the cemetery. Impressionable youngsters who visited in the sixties, however, have memories of a fearsome curator assuring them that *Magnifico* was still there in spirit *and* body. . . .

A cheery bunch of characters from the Lanarkshire Constabulary. As is the case today, nineteenth century police forces were used for strike-breaking during industrial disputes. Workers such as miners were more or less at the mercy of their wealthy employers, and conditions were often hazardous, with fatal accidents in the workplace common. During disputes, polis such as these were sent in to protect the interests of the rich.

LEITH DOCK.   RUSSELITE.   BRANDON SERIES

This postcard has a direct connection to a Quarry Street ironmongers. During the late 1880s, the shop was originally owned by one Mr Russel and Russelite, advertised on the boat here, was his brand-name explosive. Russelite would have been a carbine explosive bought by miners in quarter pound tins for use in the collieries. The Forrest family bought the business in 1916 and are still running it today. Technically, they still have the licence for the explosive, although they no longer sell it.

This 1968 picture shows Mr Forrest outside his shop, flanked by the managing directors of a promotions company. He had just won the car in a window display competition. This picture was taken by Sharp photographers, a company based a little further up the street, and at the time the ironmongers still had mahogany counters with all the goods stacked behind them.

Kings Tailors were located in Quarry Street, and this postcard was sent to a friend of the owner. The message reads: *Just a line to let you know that I'm still in the land of the living. What do you think of our new premises? I expect to get the management of it shortly. How are all at the shop? Kindly remind me to Mr Causick and Mr Littlewood, not forgetting Miss Peaslou. I can't say that I like Scotland but perhaps there's worse. Tell Causick I have not* forgotten. *The little chap is my boss. He's not so bad, makes a good chum. Don't forget to remember me to the boss and the girls. Yours as before, Harold.*

This shabbily exotic pawn shop has now been sandblasted and reborn as the Italian Connection furniture shop. Around the fifties and sixties it was Jays furniture shop, after which it was bought by Mr Pisano. Since then it has held a combination of either his own businesses or tenants ranging from the Pinnochio Restaurant, to a pizzeria, an Indian restaurant and, of course, the current furniture shop.

This picture looks up Quarry Street towards the New Cross, also known as the Top Cross. This was created in 1830 when the Edinburgh to Ayr turnpike route was joined by Duke Street and Brandon Street. Turnpikes were proper roads, such as we take for granted today, maintained by a cartel which made a tidy profit by charging a toll for its services. Toll houses were erected to collect the levy, normally on a corner junction to dissuade travellers from sneaking by without paying. Hamilton's turnpikes were apparently difficult to maintain because of the softness of the soil and the weight of the carriages using them. Despite this, carriages were able to hold three times as much weight as they had been before the advent of maintained roads.

QUARRY STREET, HAMILTON.

B.3285

Quarry Street, photographed from the Top Cross at Brandon Street. The town hall (on the far right in this picture) has met its demise, and one of the entrances to the New Cross Shopping Centre now appears on the left past the Excelsior Store (currently a branch of the Abbey National). At one time Quarry Street would have been hoaching with cattle instead of cars, due to the many cattle-pens in its vicinity. Livestock used to be driven into Castle Street near an area once known as Herrin Square because of the fish wives selling their produce there.

43

QUARRY STREET, HAMILTON.

Regent Way walkway now appears halfway down Quarry Street on the right, providing an entrance to yet another section of the shopping centre. The street has been pedestrianised to make the most of its role as principal shopping area, with benches and trees scattered along its length. William Glass, advertised on the back of the truck on the left, still has a shop in the arcade.

OLD CROSS AND QUARRY STREET, HAMILTON. B.3286.

Quarry Street was named after the Donaghadee Quarry, mentioned in records of the 1630s. Castle Street veers off to the left of the gushet in this picture, with the Douglas Bar now occupying the ground floor of Douglas Chambers (centre). What is now the Vogue Social Club appears to its right. This white brick affair arrived as La Scala Cinema in 1921 and was considered a palace by locals. Its name changed to the not very cinema-ish Gaumont in the late forties, and sure enough, it became a bingo hall twenty odd years later. The 'neck o' the bottle' at the end of the street, where people gathered at New Year, was widened in 1921. Burtons (bottom right) was originally set back from the line of buildings when it opened in the late twenties. The Cross Cafe can be made out just past it.

In the early nineteenth century, Quarter was the site of Hamilton's first mines, as well as the only blast furnaces in the area, which smelted local blackband ironstone. Until the 1850s almost all of the Dukes' mining was done at Quarter, Merryton and Avonbanks. One writer intimated that his miners were often underpaid because of the 'hutch' system. This worked on the premise that if the coal in a hutch (or tub) didn't weigh a certain amount it was forfeited. Coal was transported from Quarter by railway along the banks of the Avon to the Avon bridge, and by horse and cart thereon. In the latter decades of the nineteenth century new technology made it possible to get at previously inaccessible coal, and this church was erected in 1884 to serve the rising population. A pit at Quarter was reopened for a short time during the 1950s.

QUARTER, NEAR HAMILTON

BRANDON SERIES

Quarter was a village dominated by its mines, and the United Colliery Company ran the village store and supplied street lighting as well as paying the wages. However, there was no electricity within the room-and-kitchen colliery cottages until the 1940s. Local miners wore tackety boots, which worked as an impromptu alarm call for village residents as they marched noisily to work. The danger down the mines seemed to promote a sense of community outwith working hours, and a Welfare Hall was opened in 1910. There were other facilities for the workers such as a library and billiards hall, and special occasions would also merit dancing in the streets, according to one former resident. The miners' rows have since been cleared away and redeveloped as a modern housing scheme.

Caledonian Central Station, Hamilton.

The Caledonian Railway first arrived at Hamilton West in the late 1840s via a branch line from Newton. Hamilton Central, above, was opened some thirty odd years later when the line was extended to connect with the Lesmahagow Branch at Ross Junction. It caused great engineering difficulties, involving the construction of three bridges and the removal of huge boulders from the section parallel to John Street. By the 1950s there were two other stations, Burnbank (run by London and North Eastern Region) and the North British station which stood where St Mary's Primary School is now. The companies were amalgamated in 1948 under the umbrella of British Rail, with the two additional stations eventually closing down. British Rail standard fittings subsequently took the place of the station buildings here.

Low-Waters-Brae, Hamilton.

Low Waters was a village in its own right until it was incorporated into the Burgh in 1878, when it would have been nothing more than a row of houses. In 1862 Cadzow Colliery was sunk there, and at eight hundred feet was thought to be one of the deepest pits in the Clyde Valley. It was owned by the Cadzow Coal Company who reputedly had Keir Hardie as an employee at one point – although other mines have made similar claims.

Known as the High Parks, Cadzow Forest estate has at least two legends pertaining to its origin. Some writers maintained that the trees were planted by King David I in the twelfth century, while others thought that they were the remains of the ancient Caledonian Forest which once stretched across great tracts of Scotland. But these historians got it wrong. A ring method experiment found that the oldest oak only dated back to 1444, still an impressive age nevertheless. In the past the woods were home to Hamilton's wild, white cattle which were thought to descend from Roman times. Someone who bought this postcard named the lodge on the front as 'Hoblet Row' in a message scrawled across the back.

THE CAMERONIANS (Scottish Rifles).
(26th Foot and 90th Foot,)
BATTLE HONOURS.

The Sphinx, superscribed "Egypt." The Dragon, superscribed "China."

"Blenheim,"

"Ramillies,"

"Oudenarde,"

"Malplaquet,"

"Mandora,"

"Corunna,"

"Martinique, 1809."

"Guadaloupe, 1810."

"Sevastopol,"

"Lucknow,"

"Abyssinia,"

"South Africa, 1846-7, 1877-8-9,"

"South Africa, 1899-1902,"

"Relief of Ladysmith."

HISTORY AND TRADITIONS.

The regiment was raised in 1689. Proceeding to Flanders in 1691 it fought bravely at Steinkirk & Landen and at the famous siege of Namur. To Flanders again in 1702 it took part in Marlborough's campaigns and was present at Blenheim, Ramillies, Oudenarde, Malplaquet, and numerous other engagements. It served in the defence of Gibraltar 1726-7. It greatly distinguished itself at the siege of Alexandria in 1801. In 1808 it was present at the battle of Corunna, and later in the Walcheren Expedition, where it suffered severely. It served with much distinction throughout the first Chinese War 1840-2, and in the Kaffir War 1846-7. In the Crimean War it distinguished itself in the assault on the Redan. During the Indian Mutiny it served in the Relief of Lucknow, and in the subsequent operations. It was present in the Zulu War of 1878-9. During the South African War it formed part of Buller's Army in Natal; and performed much hard and good service, its casualties amounting to 22 Officers, and 241 men killed and wounded,

The Cameronians were a regiment descended from Covenanters. Disbanded in 1968, they have their own town museum in what was formerly the Duke's stables.

Hamilton has a long sporting background. James III tried to ban 'fute ball and golfe' because he believed they were too distracting for his subjects, and Hamiltonians were amongst those who had to practise compulsory archery instead, in their case in the grounds of the Parish Church. However, the Hamiltons seem to have been instrumental in introducing several sports to the district. They used Cadzow Forest for hunting deer in the sixteenth century and revived golf a couple of hundred years later. Bowling alleys existed in the palace grounds at the turn of the seventeenth century and horse-racing took place there from the 1780s. Modern racing began a century later, and a new track was laid in 1926 when the old one, like everything else, was hit by mining operations. This picture of a jockey was taken by Hamilton photographer John Chalmers of Chapel Street.

Hamilton Accies (right) were initially founded as a school team in 1875. At one point in the sixties they had a player by the name of Hamilton who had the distinction of scoring the most own goals in the season.

C000244860

**Towns and Villages
OF ENGLAND**

ASPATRIA

To Muriel Joan MacNab (née Glaister)
from Alfred Glaister, (Uncle).
1, Noble Croft, Aspatria

20/22 Borthyn, Denbigh Rd. Ruthin Clwyd

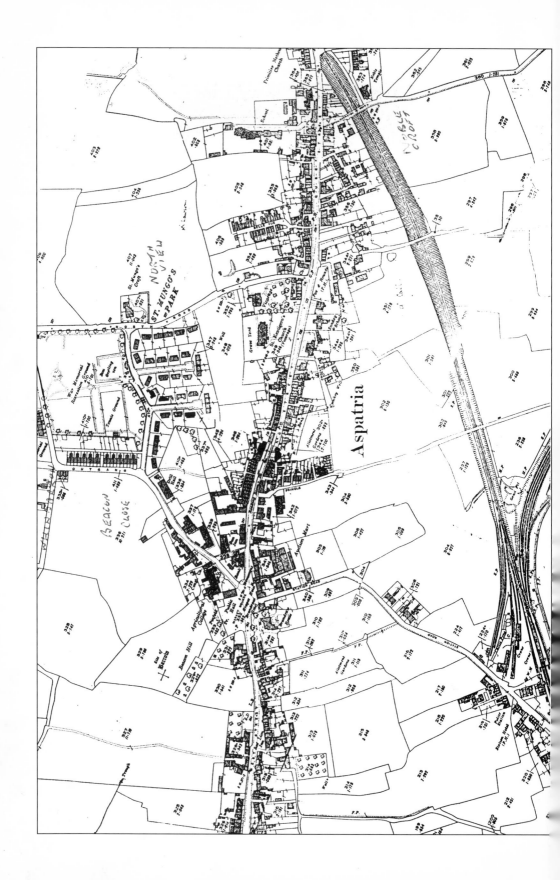

Towns and Villages
OF ENGLAND

ASPATRIA

ANNE USHER THOMAS

ALAN SUTTON

First published in the United Kingdom in 1993 by
Alan Sutton Publishing Ltd · Phoenix Mill · Far Thrupp · Stroud
Gloucestershire

First published in the United States of America in 1993 by
Alan Sutton Publishing Inc · 83 Washington Street · Dover · NH 03820

Copyright © Anne Usher Thomas, 1993

All rights reserved. No part of this publication may be reproduced, stored in a
retrieval system, or transmitted, in any form, or by any means, electronic,
mechanical, photocopying, recording or otherwise, without the prior
permission of the publishers and copyright holder.

British Library Cataloguing in Publication Data.

Thomas, Anne Usher
  Towns and Villages of England: Aspatria
  I. Title
  942.787

ISBN 0-7509-0498-4

Library of Congress Cataloging in Publication Data applied for.

Typeset in 11/13 Bembo.
Typesetting and origination by
Alan Sutton Publishing Limited.
Printed in Great Britain by
Hartnolls Ltd, Bodmin, Cornwall.

Contents

Acknowledgements

I should like to express thanks to those who have contributed in various ways to this book, first and foremost Peter W. Robinson who has spent many hours printing from the original half plate glass negatives in my collection. I am also indebted to the following for their help: Simon Thraves, Alan Sutton Publishing; J. Broughton; Len Hewitson; David Armstrong; Miss W. Douglas; W. Hoskins, Sealy UK Ltd; P. Lister IGE, Hon. Archivist of the Institute of Gas Engineers; British Gas (Northern) plc; Ken Gorley, Maryport and NORWEB plc; North West Water plc; Jennifer Reay, Larma Ltd; Trevor Jones and his staff, Workington Local Studies Library; Alan Roberts and Alistair Dodd, British Telecom plc; *West Cumberland Times* and *Star* offices, Workington and Cockermouth; Ethel Fisher, Seaton; Cumbria Record Office, Carlisle; Ordnance Survey, Southampton (for use of Aspatria map); Cumbrian Newspapers Ltd, for their kind permission to reproduce the photographs on p. 42.

And to those photographers long gone who with their foresight gave us a lasting glimpse into our past. Also, last but not least, my husband and my parents for their help and constant support.

This is a heavily illustrated history of everyday events in Aspatria. I have only briefly dealt with the early origins of the town, as that aspect has already been adequately covered by Dr Rose and Margaret Dunglinson in their book. While the information in this book to the best of my knowledge is correct, it has been interpreted from information available at this time; future discoveries in the form of documents or photographs may alter some of these findings and theories. I apologize for any errors that may have inadvertently crept in.

CHAPTER ONE

Early Days and the Church

In the beginning a settlement grew up on the site of the present small Cumbrian town of Aspatria, at the meeting place of the paths through the swamps and woods of ancient history. The settlement was on the higher ground above the valley of the River Ellen. Stone axe heads, arrow heads and other tools have been found in and around Aspatria. A monument or temple of standing stones once stood in a field at Fitz Farm. As time progressed, our pre-Christian ancestors began to bury their dead in graves on the higher ground. A Mr Rigg, of Beacon House, had a mound on his farmland excavated in 1789. This was carefully done, and a skeleton of a man 7 ft tall was uncovered. Buried with him was an elegantly ornamented great sword, a dagger, shield, helmet and spurs, all of the Viking era: these items are now in the British Museum in London. In the 1780s a fragment of an old silver brooch was found in the mud of the pond at Brayton Estate. It is known as the Brayton Fibula and resembled brooches found in Viking graves.

The Vikings invaded the Solway coast, and it is thought that the town was named by them Asc Patric, which in their language meant Patrick's Ash. However, this is not substantiated and another school of thought prefers the naming after Gos Patric, the first Earl of Northumberland. Whatever the truth the Vikings were certainly here, and many local surnames are said to be derived from this origin.

While the Battle of Hastings and later the signing of the Magna Carta were taking place, our ancestors continued to suffer constant invasions from Scotland. The last time the Scots raged through the town was during the Jacobite rebellion of 1745.

Aspatria became a royal manor in 1541, the lands being surrendered to Henry VIII by the 6th Earl of Northumberland. The manor house was at Richmond Hill. The greatest changes came in the sixteenth century with the Reformation. Holme Cultram Abbey was closed in 1543, releasing the land around Aspatria into secular ownership.

It was during this time that written records began to be kept. The parish church was ordered to have a 'sure coffer' made of sturdy oak, known as the parish chest, in which to store all the records (books, registers and documents relating to parish business), and for the safe keeping of the church silver and communion plate. It was the use of the parish chest that led to the survival of many records which are now available to family historians. The Poor Law Act of 1640 was the basis of poor law administration and until 1834 the churchwardens were the overseers of the poor. The Civil War also took its toll, leaving the area starving and destitute. During the Georgian era we see the beginning of the census returns (every ten years from 1801), although there was no great detail in the returns until 1841. We then come to the next great change – the Victorians and their industrial revolution. Their achievements in the town are dealt with in later chapters. In 1864 we see the general registration of births, marriages and deaths. The end of the nineteenth century saw the founding of local government, albeit on a more local level than we know it. Piped water, gas, sewage and many of the conveniences of modern life came into being in this era, and are dealt with in a later chapter.

The Parish Church – St Kentigern's

There has been a church on the hill at Aspatria since around AD 400, the first building probably being a small wooden structure. Before this time our ancestors would have worshipped pagan gods. It was the Romans who first brought Christianity to the people, along with their culture and talents. They left us their splendid road between Alauna (Maryport) and Carlisle, and many artefacts have been unearthed. The parish church was dedicated to St Kentigern whose emblems were the fish and the ring. He preached at the church as he passed through Aspatria on foot, on his way from his homeland in Scotland to Wales and exile. He was also known as 'Mungo', which means 'good friend'.

The Saxons and the Normans came and relics of their architecture can still be seen in the church today. The Norman church would have been built around 1100, although there is evidence in the various sculptures of the earlier Saxon church. Passing through the Middle Ages and into Tudor times the church appears to have come through unscathed, although the suffering of the people was a different matter.

Sir Walter Scott in his *Border Antiquities* of 1814 writes of the fine Norman church in Aspatria, and engravings illustrate the interior of the building.

In the early nineteenth century the old church was in a bad state of repair and the Victorians decided to rebuild it. The foundation stone was laid on 23 July 1846 with full masonic ceremonial, and the new church was consecrated on 6 June 1848. The total cost of the rebuilding, raised by grants and public subscription, was £3,180 3s 2d. The chief architectural features of the old Church were preserved, and as far as possible included in the new building. Thus a fine Norman doorway was used as the entrance to the vestry, and another was placed in the tower. The old chancel arch was erected at the west

St Kentigern's parish church

Interior of St Kentigern's parish church

The chancel of the old Norman church
from an engraving in Sir Walter Scott's
Border Antiquities of 1814

Norman arch over the vestry door

end of the church, between the vestry and the tower. A chapel to the Musgrave family was restored. The old font dates from before the Reformation, when it was defaced and thrown out as useless. It lay in the churchyard until it was 'discovered' and restored during the building work of 1846–8. A new central pillar with four others surrounding it formed the support for the font, the whole being mounted on an octagonal base. The holes, made in the font at the Reformation, were filled and the decorative carving restored. It was placed under the west arch in the new church, and remained there until it was moved into the baptistry in 1903. Also in the baptistry are part of an ancient 'hog back' or stone coffin, which was found in the churchyard, and a list of all the priests who have served Aspatria since around 1174. Decorative stone carvings from earlier churches were built into parts of the walls, especially in the vestry. Many of the beautiful stained glass windows from the old church were incorporated in the new, together with some new stained glass dedicated to local families and coal owners.

6 January 1875 saw the dedication of a new organ presented to the church by Sarah Langcake at a cost of £200, the installation of which required major alterations to the chancel as provision had not been made for an organ in the rebuilding of 1846–8. At the same time a fine brass chandelier, the gift of Lady Lawson, was hung in the chancel at a cost of £40. A year later Mrs Powell, the widow of an earlier vicar, paid for a clock to be placed in the tower as a memorial to her husband. She also paid for one of the bells, when the parishioners in 1898 realized their wish to have a peal of eight bells in the tower. Lady Lawson and her friends paid for three more, the children of the parish raised money for another and the remainder were paid for by a bazaar and sale of work. Putting heating into the church cost £221 in 1899.

The year of 1903 saw the church requiring major restoration, which cost over £900, after a violent storm in March of that year had loosened stones on the top of the spire and caused other structural damage. At the same time the organ chamber was extended and the wall paintings in the chancel were done by Mr G. Goodall, a local painter and decorator. The superb oak gates at the King Street entrance to the church were hand carved by Mr Joseph Berwick in 1933. As with most elderly buildings the church is in need of constant repair and restoration, the more urgent work being carried out after each quinquennial inspection by the church's architects. Raising the money for repairs is a never-ending task for the members of the church.

The hog back coffin, St Kentigern's

The font, St Kentigern's

The west door, St Kentigern's, with the reproduction of a Norman arch – Victorian craftsmanship

St Kentigern's church: gates made by Joe Berwick, at the main entrance on King Street

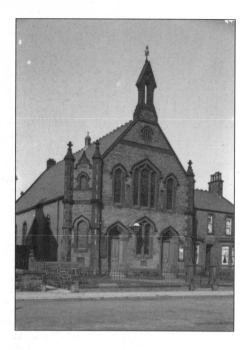

Primitive Methodist church and manse, Queen Street

THE NON-CONFORMIST CHAPELS OF ASPATRIA

Primitive Methodists

The original Primitive Methodist chapel was built in Lawson Street in 1866, and continued in use as a Sunday School after the new Primitive Methodist chapel and its manse were built on Queen Street next to the railway bridge in 1896, at a cost of £1,280. It was a fine building, built of grey Lazonby stone set off with red sandstone dressings, buttressed and surmounted by a bell tower. The interior had a gallery and seating for 350 people. Kathleen Ferrier, the renowned contralto, sang in the chapel and the fine organ was used for a concert by Sandy MacPherson, of BBC radio fame. Sadly, this building is no more. After the Primitive Methodists and Wesleyans joined together in 1976 they used the Wesleyan Hall at the corner of Queen Street and North Road for worship. The Primitive Methodist chapel was used by the Roman Catholic church for a few years and then demolished. The manse survives as a private house, and a new dwelling was built on the site of the chapel. The organ was carefully removed to the Wesleyan Hall and is still in use to this day. The old chapel on Lawson Street outlived its replacement and still survives, but in a derelict state.

The original Wesleyan chapel at the corner of North Road and Queen Street

The celebration tea for the opening of the new Wesleyan chapel in the Co-op Hall, King Street, 4 April 1929

Congregational chapel, Outgang, near Market Square

Richmond Hill chapel (Baptists)

It was in August 1883 that the Christian Brethren, or Baptists as they are better known, began to build their chapel on the corner of Queen Street and Richmond Hill. It was completed in 1886 at a cost of £800. Before the building of the chapel they had used the Noble Temple for worship. In front of the altar and covered by removable flooring was a well, which was used for total immersion baptism. In 1894 an evening's entertainment was given in the chapel by Messrs Overs String Band, with Charles at the organ and John as leader. When the chapel closed, the building became the Primitive Methodist Sunday School and Youth Club until the Methodists joined with the Wesleyans. Pat Scott of Silloth then used the building as a furniture shop for a few years before it was demolished and a private dwelling was built on the site, aptly named Chapel House.

Wesleyan Hall

An early photograph shows the original place of worship, which was built at the junction of North Road and Queen Street in 1898. A new Wesleyan Hall was built on the site in the late 1920s, the new building being dedicated and consecrated at a service on 4 April 1929, when the preacher and speaker was the Revd F. Luke Wiseman, a former president of the Methodist Conference. After the service tea was served in the Co-operative Hall, King Street, and a photograph shows the room laid out for the occasion. The Wesleyans held their services in the Co-operative Hall while the new building was built by Messrs Davidson and Beattie, Aspatria builders. When the Primitive Methodist chapel closed in 1976 it was to the Wesleyan Hall that their fine organ was moved, and they joined together in worship.

Congregational chapel

Built in 1827, this was the first of the Non-conformist chapels to be built in the town. On Outgang Road, the chapel had accommodation for about three hundred persons. It remained in use for over 100 years until being taken over by a spectacle factory, and it now stands empty and neglected. The Congregationalists had their own cemetery further along Outgang Road, opened in 1851. The land was the gift of Sir Wilfred Lawson for use of the chapel congregation only, and some members of the Lawson family are buried there.

CHAPTER TWO

Manor of Brayton and the Estate

The Manor of Brayton is part of the present parish of Aspatria. It was given by Alan, 2nd Lord of Allerdale, to Uchtred, who also held Uchtredby (Oughterside) and whose descendants took the name of Brayton. In 1255 we find the name Breyton, which may be compounded of the Norse, bried (broad), and the Anglo Saxon, ton (town or farm); or it may be merely the 'abode of Brahe'.

By the inquisition of 1578, William Bewley held the manor by fealty only, it having been at some time the lands of the Bishop of Carlisle in free alms. The estate came into the possession of the younger branches of the Salkeld family, whose three co-heiresses in the early part of the eighteenth century sold it to Sir Wilfred Lawson. Until the fire of August 1918 destroyed the house, Brayton Hall remained the home of the Lawson family. The family then moved to Isel Hall, Cockermouth, on another of the family estates.

BRAYTON ESTATE AND THE LAWSON FAMILY

When the Lawsons took over Brayton Estate it is said to have consisted of 1,503 acres, three-quarters of which was ancient woodland. A century later young plantations were formed, including many birch trees, whose wood was much in demand for the soles of clogs. A little later the planting of oak was increased for eventual use in shipbuilding.

The lodges to the Hall can still be seen today, and the photographs show two of the lodges as they were at the turn of the century. Luckily photographs remain of this beautiful mansion showing the Hall at the turn of the century, the building being virtually rebuilt after being purchased by the Lawsons. There are also fine views of the lake. During the early part of the twentieth century Brayton Hall grounds and gardens were open to the public on alternate Sunday afternoons.

The Hall also had its own railway station, the lodge at the approach to the Hall being aptly named 'Station Lodge'. This was on the main road to Carlisle. Railway excursions were run to Brayton station for people who were visiting the Hall and grounds.

Jubilee Lodge, Brayton Road

Station Lodge

There were large stables at the Hall and photographs show them during Sir Wilfred's time. Initialled horse blankets, the Lawson crests and plaited straw on the floor can all be seen. During the Second World War part of the Brayton Estate was closed off and used as an emergency airfield.

When the estate was disposed of and broken up for sale, the kitchen gardens became a commercial nursery known as Brayton Gardens, run firstly by Mr Irving and then by Mr John Ben Holliday, and was renowned for its excellent produce. Later it was purchased by Jim and Dorothy Armstrong who continued the business until they retired, after which the land was developed into a small private housing estate.

SIR WILFRED LAWSON, 2ND BARONET OF BRAYTON AND ISEL
1829–1906

It seems strange that Sir Wilfred Lawson was not really a Lawson at all. The original Lawson family was descended from an old Yorkshire family, which first came to Cumberland through the marriage of Sir Wilfred Lawson Bt to the widow of Thomas Leigh of Isel Hall, near Cockermouth. In the early 1700s they purchased the Brayton Estate from a branch of the Salkeld family. Many generations of the Lawsons lived on the estate and in 1806 the last of the line, Sir Wilfred Lawson, died without a direct heir to his title. The estate passed to Wilfred, son of Thomas Wybergh, who had married Lady Lawson's sister, with the proviso that the boy should change his name to Lawson. So our Sir Wilfred's father was known as Sir Wilfred Wybergh Lawson, his father Thomas Wybergh occupying Isel Hall.

'Our' Sir Wilfred (the 2nd Baronet), as he was known to the people of Aspatria, was born in 1829. He married Miss Mary Pocklington-Senhouse of Netherhall, Maryport in 1860. They lived at Arkleby Hall on the Cockermouth road until they moved to Brayton Hall on the death of the first Baronet Lawson in 1879. He was a staunch Liberal and, as his father had been before him, a total abstainer from alcohol. It is said that when his father inherited Brayton Hall he ordered that the contents of the wine cellar should be poured into the lake on the estate.

Sir Wilfred was first President of the Aspatria Agricultural College, Chairman of the Maryport and Carlisle Railway from 1874 until 1906, Chairman of the Quarter Sessions at Carlisle, Member of Parliament for the Carlisle constituency from 1859 and later for the Cockermouth constituency of Cumberland, and Master of the Foxhounds. He began his hunting career in 1850 in West Cumberland with the legendary John Peel, often hunting with him, and keeping a few hounds of his own. After John Peel's death Sir Wilfred (or Mr Lawson as he was then) became the owner of the entire pack

Brayton Pond, a favourite place for skating in the winter

Main entrance to Brayton Hall

Brayton Hall, home of Sir Wilfred Lawson, MP

The stables, Brayton Hall. Note the monogrammed horse blankets

Sir Wilfred Lawson Bart, MP

Funeral cortège of Sir Wilfred Lawson in Queen Street, Thursday 5 July 1906

Entries for the competition for the design of a memorial to Sir Wilfred Lawson, held in the Public Hall

The memorial to Sir Wilfred Lawson, designed by L. Fritz Roselieb

of hounds, and from these were formed the second and third packs of Cumberland foxhounds, though they were not formally named as such until 1859. A walk along Brayton Road and past the kennels was a favourite Sunday walk for many Aspatarians.

Sir Wilfred's role in the beginning of the Agricultural College is outlined later, as is his involvement with the Maryport and Carlisle Railway. It makes one wonder what Aspatria would have been like if there had been no Sir Wilfred Lawson – he was a true benefactor of the town and a great man. I'm sure he would have approved of the Waverley Temperance Hotel in King Street.

Sir Wilfred and Lady Lawson were involved in too many local activities and charitable acts to mention, and there were many things done that no one knew about. For example, Lady Lawson paid the school fees for the children of the estate workers: the author's grandmother's education was paid for in this way.

Sir Wilfred Lawson died on 1 July 1906 in London, his body was brought home to Brayton, and the funeral took place on 5 July 1906 at St Kentigern's church with, as can be seen in the photographs, tremendous crowds descending on the town, people coming from all over the county and country to pay their last respects to this great man. He was buried in St Kentigern's

Crowds at the official dedication of the memorial

Floral tributes at Sir Wilfred Lawson's funeral

graveyard and his tomb is there for all to see. The photographs show the cortège moving through the town and his gravestone with all the funeral flowers still *in situ*.

For one who had done so much good for the town it was decided to erect a monument to his memory in the Market Square. There were many entries for the design of the monument, as can be seen in the photograph taken in the Market Hall where all the entries were exhibited and the winner chosen. The monument, on land given by the College, was unveiled on 21 April 1908 and photographs show the large crowd that gathered to witness this event. Another memorial was erected in London, this time a statue of the great man.

CHAPTER THREE

Aspatria Agricultural College

The College was founded in 1874 for the purpose of affording a thorough instruction in the scientific principles of agriculture and land management to future farmers, land agents and others.

The College had a thriving journal known as *Aspatria Agricultural College Chronicle*, which reported on the life of the College, its students past and present. How the College was first started and its early days I will leave in the capable hands of Mr Henry Thompson MRCVS, the Aspatria veterinary surgeon, who described the founding in a speech he gave to the College prize giving on Friday 20 July 1906 in the Market Hall, Aspatria. The *College Chronicle* reported it thus:

I will briefly refer to the early connection of the late Sir Wilfred Lawson with the Aspatria Agricultural College. In 1869, at the first agricultural show in Aspatria, Sir Wilfred in his after dinner speech, strongly recommended the cooperation of farmers. His recommendation was acted upon with the result that in the year following the Aspatria Agricultural Society was formed, and I have had the honour of acting as Secretary since its formation. Mr William Norman, having had a scientific education at Cirencester Agricultural College, was a leader in its formation. Mr Twentyman was so much interested in Mr Norman's scientific work that he conceived the idea of establishing an agricultural college or school in the North [of England] for the benefit of tenant farmers. The late Sir Wilfred Lawson was approached on the subject, and he invited the late Mr John Todd of Mereside [father of Mrs Smith-Hill], the late Mr J. Grainger of Southerfield, the late Mr John Carson of Round Hill, his brother Mr William Carson of Foulsyke, Mr Norman, Mr Twentyman and myself to Brayton to afternoon tea, and there the scheme of establishing an agricultural school at Aspatria was floated with an issue of one pound shares, and was called the Aspatria Agricultural School Company Limited. Sir Wilfred at the same time let the promoters have what is now known as the Temperance Lecture Hall as a place to teach. The first three pupils were the present Mr Jos Barnes of Baurgh; his brother Mr J.W. Barnes of Aikbank (the well known shorthorn breeders); and the late Mr William Barnes of Mowbray. As the school progressed, larger accommodation was required and the property of Beacon House coming on to the market, was purchased. Owing to large alterations having to be done which the share capital would not cover, the late Sir Wilfred was bound for £2,100 on his own part and others of the directors a further £1,000 and as time went on other requirements were wanted, and the school was generally in difficulties, and the late Sir Wilfred was often called on to back up the concern until the pupils' fees could be collected. A number of influential gentlemen acted on the directorate and on one occasion a meeting was held at Wigton when I, as secretary, laid before the meeting a statement of the financial position of the school, when my friend Mr James Watt of Carlisle looked over the statement and remarked that the concern was insolvent, and proposed that it be wound up. I then said that the school was as solvent and in as good a position as it ever had been, and unless Mr Watt and the seconder could see their way to recoup Sir Wilfred and the other directors for the bonds they were standing under, it was no use closing up the place. Sir Wilfred asked, 'What would you suggest, Thompson?' My reply was that the whole of the directors should sign a bond at the bank for any overdraft that might be required and we should sail the ship again. Sir Wilfred said he liked the idea better than winding up the school and offered to go for £250 himself if the other directors would go for another £250. Mr Foster and Mr Banks of Highmoor offered to stand for the second amount, but subsequently it was arranged that the whole body of directors would sign a bond for the £500 required. After that Mr Watt became uneasy and he never rested until he got clear of the bond by selling the College to Dr Webb. I venture to say if it had not been for the late Sir Wilfred Lawson, there would have been no Aspatria Agricultural College today [1906].

Included in the *Chronicle* reports were meetings of the Old Aspatrian Club (the old boys), and each year details were given of the annual meeting and dinner held initially in London, but later at the Crown and Mitre Hotel, Carlisle. In the September 1906 edition details were given regarding the gift of land by the college for the purpose of erecting a memorial to Sir Wilfred Lawson (2nd Baronet), who had died that July. Former students of the College wrote from all over the world as well as from all parts of Great Britain, telling how they were progressing and using the knowledge acquired while attending the school.

The Agricultural College

Accommodation for the boarding students was at Yarra House, Linden House and Jersey Cottage on King Street in the town. There were six farms connected with the college to enable the students to carry out practical work, one being the Mechi Model Farm built by William Lawson on the outskirts of Blennerhassett village. This farm was laid out on the most up-to-date farming principles of the time. A laboratory was built at the West Cumberland Dairy Co. for the use of the College.

The College finally closed its doors to students in 1925. The buildings were used for many different purposes until they were demolished in 1962. The Beacon Hill Secondary School and a new library for the town were erected on the site in 1962.

CHAPTER FOUR

Coal Mining and other Industries

COAL MINING

In the dim and distant past much of the land which forms the County of Cumberland was covered with forests. Marshland, swamps and bogs covered the lower land, especially in the river valleys between the mountains and the sea. It is these once wet areas that now form the West Cumberland coalfield, which stretches from south of Whitehaven to just north of Aspatria. There was also a rich iron ore deposit in the west of the county, overlapping with the coal south of Whitehaven. Mining began in the Aspatria area as early as 1657 with drift mines, and many coalfields were developed over the next 250 years. The Duke of Somerset sank pits at Oughterside in 1681, and Sir Wilfred Lawson opened a mine in the area – but was unable to make it pay due to the cheap price of coal from the Bolton Colliery. Pits were operated in this area right up to the early 1900s and even in the 1980s the area had opencast mining. Bolton Colliery was visited by Bishop Nicholson in 1707, and workings in the area lasted until 1869. Maryport Iron Company (which eventually became part of the 'combine', as the Workington Iron & Steel Company was known) took over the lease and opened up again at Bolton in 1872. It continued to mine, selling its coal locally and sending to its works at Maryport, via the Bolton branch of the Maryport and Carlisle Railway. Until the opening of the railway all coal had to be transported by road. In the mid-eighteenth century the Lawsons wanted to cut a canal from the River Ellen to Blue Dial near Allonby for ease of shipment. These aspirations came to nothing as landowners objected to the canal passing through their land. The area is honeycombed with mine-workings; the road between Prospect and Westmoor End was once level but now has many hills and hollows. All-hallows Colliery was sunk in 1874, closing down in 1902; Baggrow Knowe on Brayton Estate land was opened in 1902, closing fifteen years later in 1917. Brayton Domain is the best known of the collieries, Nos 1 and 2 being situated behind the site of the present industrial estate by the railway station. These were sunk by Joseph Harris in the 1850s, and both closed in 1870. Other pits followed. Harris's No. 3 pit at Harriston was sunk in 1868 and remained in production until 1902. The accident rate was dreadful: in the 1880s one accident every week was being reported, many of them fatal. Photographs show the pit workings close to the village, towards the end and during demolition of No. 3 pit.

In 1890 No. 4 pit was opened near to Brayton station. Known as Wellington Pit it was lit by electricity in 1898, and continued to be worked until 1933. Mr Harris sank his final pit, No. 5, between 1907 and 1910; this was situated alongside the railway to the south of the station between Aspatria and Ellen Villa. The pit finally closed in 1942. The photographs of Nos 4 and 5 collieries show both the surface and underground. Mining was a hard and hazardous life, with long hours and cramped dirty conditions both for the men and the pit ponies. Some of the shots were taken while No. 5 pit was being sunk and before any coal was brought to the surface, the obviously new condition of the tipplers and lack of coal on the floor bearing witness to this.

Harriston is the colliery village built next to No. 3 pit by Mr Harris the pit owner. At one time it had its own Co-op store, mission hall, infant school and recreation rooms. The Harriston Bowling Club had a fine green, as can also be seen in the photograph. The closeness of the village to the pit can also be seen. The old village was demolished in the 1970s and a new Harriston was built by the local authority.

Oughterside Pit, Aspatria Coal Company

Brayton Domain No. 3 pit at Harriston:
Beehive coke ovens

Pit buildings at No. 3 pit being prepared for demolition

One chimney falls at No. 3 pit

Another chimney falls at No. 3 pit

'All fall down' at No. 3 pit

Sidings at No. 4 (Wellington) pit with chaldron wagons on the left

No. 4 pit, with *Sir Hugh* awaiting work

The author's great grandfather, Joseph Douglas, on the right, underground at No. 4 pit

Will Dobie shovelling coal at No. 4 pit

MINERS AT WORK - NO. 4 PIT, BRAYTON COLLIERIES

At the face in No. 4 pit

Hard work at the face

'Speattry' lasses on the 'jiggers' (picking belts)

Coal to the shaft at No. 4 pit

Heavy load for a pit pony

'Putters' and their ponies

A wash after a hard day's work

'Home sweet home': underground stables at No. 4 pit. Note the cats

Chaldron wagons in sidings at No. 4 pit

Brayton Domain No. 5 pit, a view of the pithead

No. 5 pit, Brayton Domain

The construction crew who sank No. 5 pit shaft

In the drift at No. 5 pit

Tipplers at No. 5 pit, before it began coal production

Brand new winding engine at No. 5 pit

Unused 'jiggers' at No. 5 pit

Digging out the main arch and winding shaft, 350 yards deep. Diggers are completing the sump at the bottom of the new shaft at No. 5 pit

Up to the top by bucket at No. 5 pit

New underground cable haulage engine at No. 5 pit

Cable haulage underground at No. 5 pit

Cable 'snatcher' at No. 5 pit

OTHER INDUSTRIES

Cumberland Federal Co-op Society had a bakery, that on Monday February 1948 went into full production, supplying bread to fourteen of the local Co-operative societies in the area. The premises were built on the site of the old Brayton Domain No. 5 pit and the delivery vehicles were to be serviced by the Motor Trade department of the Co-operative Wholesale Society (the CWS was a partner in the bakery), which was opened alongside the new bakery.

Larma Ltd is a subsidiary of the clothing manufacturer R.H. Lowe and Co., of Congleton, Cheshire. It started operations in May 1945 using temporary premises for training purposes while a new factory was built by the West Cumberland Development Company (now known as English Estates). Larma used the unemployed and old folks' recreation rooms on Queen Street, taking over the use of 'Tosh' Holliday's telephone. It was said at the time that Tosh made better sprints to fetch the staff to incoming calls than he ever did in his rugby playing days for Aspatria, Cumberland, England and Oldham RLFC. As more space was required Larma moved into part of the old Agricultural College building, the company eventually moving into its spacious new factory in October 1947. The official opening by Harold Wilson, the then President of the Board of Trade, took place on Wednesday 25 August 1948. At this time, Larma employed 210 women and girls and a dozen men, although there was room for a further 100 women. The factory produced on average 12,000 garments per working week, and clothes have been made for many famous labels since that time. The factory created much needed employment in the area following the war.

M. Hackney & Co. first began production in premises at Wigton and Maryport in 1945, moving to Aspatria in 1947 on completion of splendid new premises on the Ellen Vale site, developed by the West Cumberland Development Company. 'The Hackney', as it is known, produces top quality beds and spring interior mattresses.

The company became part of the Littlewoods organization, and in 1975 was acquired by the Silentnight Group, which was owned by an American manufacturer, Sealy of Ohio. Following this acquisition Sealy UK was formed, and the Aspatria factory is now known as Sealy of Aspatria, an acknowledged leader in the manufacturing of beds and spring interiors.

The West Cumberland Dairy Company was proposed at a meeting in the Market Hall in February 1888, and agreement was given to go ahead on the 24th of that month. It was to be built on land near the railway station and leased from Sir Wilfred Lawson, who along with Messrs Thompson, Storey, Grainger, Donald and Huddart were the first directors of the company. The building, which was specially designed for the purpose by Mr Stephenson

Official opening of Larma Ltd by Harold Wilson, President of the Board of Trade

Interior of Larma Ltd

Staff at the Milk Marketing Board unloading milk in the 1930s

from Norfolk, a dairy consultant engineer, was completed by December 1888 at a cost of £548 16s 6d and officially opened by Sir Wilfred Lawson on 9 February 1889. Aspatria Industrial Co-op had the sole agency for the sale of its products. Two brands of butter were made, Daisy and Buttercup, the former being the favourite; perhaps the milk from Sir Wilfred's famous Daisy herd of cows at Brayton was used. The dairy, a farmers' co-operative, only lasted a few years and was taken over by Carrick's Butter Company from Brampton, near Carlisle. When the Milk Marketing Board was formed in May 1934 it took over Carrick's premises at Low Row, Brampton and Aspatria. At first the MMB concentrated its work at Brampton but soon realized that the Aspatria dairy was more central for milk collection. The Aspatria MMB Dairy prospered, specializing in the production of cheeses. Dairy Crest, a subsidiary of the MMB, took over the running of the dairy in 1987, and Aspatria now has one of the most up-to-date cheese making plants in Europe.

CHAPTER FIVE

Public Services

LOCAL COUNCIL

The first local council came into being after the Local Government Act of 1871 led to the formation of the Aspatria Local Board. Further acts of Parliament in 1888 and 1894 gave Aspatria the status of an urban district, and the first council was elected in 1895. It continued to be responsible for local affairs until the much larger Wigton Rural District Council was formed in 1934. A parish council with much reduced powers came into being to take care of local matters and keep people interested in local affairs. The parish council lasted until the great local government upheaval of 1974, when the town council came into being – with permission to appoint its own mayor.

LOCAL EDUCATION

Before 1825 schooling for the children of Aspatria was limited and often intermittent, as the small school in the town was often closed because of fever epidemics. When the Lawson family purchased the Brayton Estate Sir Wilfred took an interest in the schooling of the children, although it was said that this did little other than prepare the pupils for a life of toil on the estate or on the farms around the town. In 1825 the National School was built opposite the church on the Main Street, with places for about 150 children. At the same time there were many small private schools in the town with one or two teachers.

The Elementary Education Act of 1870 led to the formation of the Aspatria and Brayton School Board. According to the newspapers of the time, much bickering took place between various religious and lay interests for places on the Board. Agreement could not be reached on the form the religious instruction would take. All this dissension prevented the Board from being formed until 1875. One of its first tasks was to deal with the overcrowding of the classes. The National School building was enlarged in 1877, but this was a temporary solution. The newly formed School Board was soon to have a new school built on the top of Richmond Hill. This Board School opened in 1895 and the old National School building was used

A school photograph with Mr James Cobb, headmaster, taken 21 September 1921

An earlier school photograph, *c.* 1919

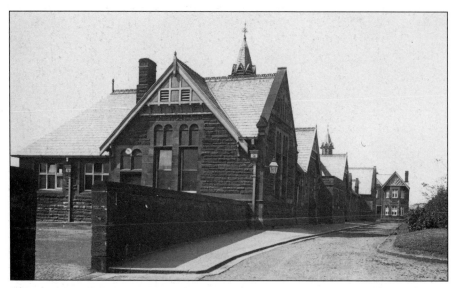

Aspatria Board School, Richmond Hill, still in use today

as a Sunday school by the parish church. The Richmond Hill Board School educated its pupils until they left school for a working life. It became the Aspatria Infant and Junior School in 1962 when a new secondary school was built at Beacon Hill, on the site of the old Agricultural College. Children requiring a grammar school education travelled to the Thomlinson Girls' School and the Nelson Boys' School at Wigton. These schools were combined in 1951, forming the Nelson Thomlinson Grammar School.

The Aspatria Agricultural College has been dealt with in an earlier chapter.

LOCAL PUBLIC SERVICES

The local services are taken for granted today, and this chapter traces the origins of some of them, bringing them up to the present time.

Water

In 1899 Mr F. Richardson, an Aspatria solicitor and Mr Richard Pickering, a civil engineer from Whitehaven, began the long road to get their Bill for the Overwater and Ellen Water Scheme approved by Parliament. The Bill passed the Select Committee of the House of Commons on 13 June 1901 and received the Royal Assent on 3 July 1901. At the next meeting of the Aspatria Rural District Council on 9 July 1901 the council appointed four

Filters at Quarry Hill Water Works, Aspatria and Silloth Water Board

representatives on the Aspatria, Silloth and District Joint Water Board, the inaugural meeting of which took place on 31 July 1901 in Bank Chambers, King Street, Aspatria.

Brayton Hall was the first place to receive the new water supply in August 1903 followed by Brayton Domain Colliery Company's No. 4 pit. It wasn't until October 1903 that the water supply arrived in the town, and only 100 houses were connected to it during the first few months – much to the concern of Dr Briggs, the local Medical Officer of Health, who was worried about the amount of sewage pollution leaking into the wells still being used by many householders. However, all 100 houses in Harriston, owned by the Colliery Company, were connected from the very beginning. In August 1911 the Board resolved to build a treatment works on land they had purchased at Quarry Hill, Boltongate, together with a house for the caretaker. Four mechanical filters were installed and a reservoir was constructed on the site, the whole costing £10,000. Later, in the mid-1920s, a reservoir was built at Chapel House, Uldale, collecting water from Skiddaw, Blencathra and the streams flowing from them. The Aspatria, Silloth and District Water Board and other local water companies were merged into the West Cumberland Water Board. The Water Board is now part of North West Water plc, and the treatment plant has recently been upgraded to give a very high quality of drinking water.

Pumps at Quarry Hill treatment plant

Interior at Quarry Hill treatment plant

Electricity

At a meeting of the Aspatria Urban District Council on 13 October 1919 it was suggested that the possibility of lighting the town by electricity should be looked into, due to the high cost of gas lighting. A figure of £143 for lighting sixty lamps was given for the winter of that year. The committee agreed that an experienced electrician should be asked to look into the matter, and that the Aspatria Gas Light Company be advised. It was not uncommon in the early days of electric lighting for the Councils, and other large users of gas, to threaten to change to the new power source in order to receive cheaper rates from the gas supplier.

Where the Council hoped to obtain their electricity from in 1919 was not stated in the newspaper report of the above meeting, for it was not until late 1932 that an electricity supply reached Aspatria. Perhaps they thought they could obtain supplies from Brayton No. 4 pit, which was electrically lit in 1898. The Co-op was another of the businesses to install their own supply before the mains supply reached the town.

The Mid-Cumberland Electricity Company, who brought the supply to the town, had their offices in High Sands Lane, Cockermouth. The electricity was supplied to Cockermouth from the National Grid sub-station at Stainburn, near Workington. The supply was switched on at Cockermouth on 15 October 1932. Towards the end of that year the supply was brought from Cockermouth to Aspatria via wooden poles and overhead wires. The Electricity Company was taken over by various larger companies until finally, at nationalization in 1948, it became part of the North Western Electricity Board's No. 7 sub-area, based at Kendal.

Telephone

The telephone was initially introduced to Aspatria in 1891, although on a somewhat limited service, by the National Telephone Company. The directory for that year lists only one subscriber – Mr F. Richardson, a solicitor. By 1895 the Aspatria exchange had been merged with Maryport and remained that way until 1912. The only Aspatria subscriber in the 1895 directory was the Allerdale Coal Company. In 1912 the Post Office took over the holdings of the National Telephone Company and in 1922 opened an exchange in Aspatria that had nineteen lines and twenty-five subscribers, some of the lines being shared. This manual exchange was replaced between March 1945 and March 1946 with an automatic exchange, which enabled calls to be made without the assistance of the operator. At that time there were 108 exchange lines with 143 telephones connected. The 999 emergency service was introduced to Aspatria subscribers between March 1957 and March 1958, and the speaking clock became available the following year. Subscriber Trunk Dialling (STD) was introduced between March 1972 and March 1973, with the building of a new exchange – the number of local subscribers having grown to 300 business lines and 238 residential customers.

The following list of customers from the 1922 Directory is of great interest; some of these numbers are still being used by the same subscribers today, albeit with prefixes. For example, Aspatria police station is now Aspatria 20210.

Post Office 1
Holliday Robinson, Queen Street 2
Manchester & Liverpool District Bank 3
G.H. Askew, Castlemont 4
No. 5 Pit, Brayton Domain 5
Aspatria Industrial Co-op Society 6
Aspatria Agricultural Co-op Society 7
Thompson & Noble Provision Merchants 8
Oughterside Coal Company 9
Police Station, Station Road 10
Thos. Ostle, Auctioneer, Outgang 11
H. & T. Bouch, 2A King Street, Motor Agents 12
I. Watson & Sons, Queen Street 13
Railway Station (M. & C. Rly) 14
Over & Sons, Motor Engineers 15
Carricks Dairy Company Ltd 16
Allhallows Colliery, Mealsgate 17
No. 4 Pit, Brayton Domain 18
Urban District Council Offices 19
Hopes Auction Co., Market Square 20

The Aspatria Gas Light Company Limited

The company was formed in 1859 with a paid up share capital of £6,000 and supplied gas, principally for lighting, to the town and the village of Harriston. Gas was made by the carbonization of coal in closed retorts, the resulting product being purified to remove tar, ammonia, napthalene and various sulphur compounds before being metered and supplied to the public. The supply was often interrupted when demand exceeded the available gas from the retorts, and the flame would burn low. This problem was done away with when a gasholder was installed in 1895. This could supply gas, on demand, via a simple governor to the street mains. In December 1903 a lighting experiment took place, whereby one lamp was fitted with the new incandescent gas light mantles, which were being used in Keswick at the time. It was found to give a brilliant light compared to the old system, and used less gas than the old 'fishtail' burners. In 1910 the total number of consumers was 627, of whom 391 were equipped with 'penny-in-the-slot' meters. Gas was also supplied to seventy-three public lamps, of which forty-eight were the more modern 'incandescent' type. In 1910 the total length of the gas mains was 3 miles.

The Company Office was located at the gasworks on Lawson Street and there were eventually two gasholders. It became a Limited Company in 1895.

The Gas Light Company continued to operate independently right up to nationalization, when on 1 May 1949 it became part of the Northern Gas Board. With the rationalization of gas production into larger units in the major towns, high pressure gas grid systems were laid to connect these units and to supply gas in bulk to the smaller communities, and as a result the local gasworks closed. This was the case with Aspatria when the high pressure main was laid between Carlisle and Workington via Wigton and Aspatria, enabling the Aspatria gasworks to cease production in 1955–6. With the introduction of natural gas a pipeline was laid in 1967 between Carlisle, Workington and Whitehaven, initially supplying 'town gas', and then natural gas when the Cumbria area was converted in 1969–70.

If there were gas lamps there had to be a lamplighter, and Bob Bell was photographed at work in King Street in the early 1900s. The job of lighting the lamps was carried on by Len Hewitson and his father until the coming of the electric street lights. On a good day, Len reckoned he could get around the lot (ninety-three lamps) in just over an hour. The cast-iron gas lamps in the town were made by a Mr Bray; hence the gas lamp at the Market Square, and its modern electric replacement have always been known to Aspatarians as the 'Bray Lamp'. It is the scene of merrymaking at New Year and other festivities.

Fire Service

The Aspatria Volunteer Fire Brigade was formed following two great fires at Mechi and Heathfield farms in the early 1870s. A meeting of the Volunteer Fire Brigade on 29 August 1874 was told that the ground next to the Aspatria Co-op had been purchased and the new engine shed was all but completed. However, insufficient funds had been received to cover the cost. On 23 October 1874, the brigade, which consisted of forty men, was invited to Brayton Hall to show their skills with the fire-fighting equipment. This

Aspatria Volunteer Fire Brigade, twenty-first birthday celebrations on 5 October 1895, outside the fire station on King Street

practice became an annual event. Sir Wilfred, along with Mr George Moore of Whitehall, Mealsgate, and Mr J.P. Foster of Killhow, Boltongate, were co-trustees of the Fire Brigade's property.

The first call-out for the new brigade was to Brayton Hall on 1 June 1875, when there was a fire in the laundry room. Until September 1875, when a fire bell was installed, the brigade was summoned by the church bell. In June 1881 the fire station was rebuilt and heightened at a cost of £41, the reason being that the Aspatria Co-op had built its cottages the previous year, and as they were much higher than the fire station the fire bell couldn't be heard. During this period anyone sending for the fire brigade was responsible for the cost of hiring the horses to pull the fire engine and any incidental expenses. The firemen themselves were responsible for the cost of their own uniforms (which often they couldn't afford) and many a volunteer ruined his Sunday Best suit after being called out to a fire while in church. There was no means to recompense him for his loss.

The splendid picture of the fire brigade was taken on 5 October 1895 on the occasion of the twenty-first anniversary of its founding. There were visiting detachments from Carlisle and Keswick, and the parade consisted of the Aspatria Fire Brigade Band, followed by the fire engine, the firemen from Aspatria and the visiting brigades on foot. At the rear a fine coach and four, kindly loaned by the Keswick visitors, carried veterans and patrons of the brigade including A.B. Clarke and G.H. Askew. Captain Topping, foreman Graham and engineer Wilson can be seen on the town engine waving flags. The glittering helmets and smart metropolitan style uniforms were lent for the day by Messrs Merryweather & Sons, engine builders of London. The celebrations continued with competitions on the cricket field at Outgang with hundreds of spectators, and afterwards a knife and fork supper for all in the National School was kindly given by Mr A.B. Clarke of Prospect House. Police uniform of the time can also be seen, two officers on the left of the photograph wearing pill-box hats. The nearer policeman has a St John's Ambulance Brigade badge on his right sleeve showing his proficiency in first aid.

The stone plaque above the doorway can still be seen over the door of the second headquarters, at Market Square, which the brigade moved into in 1905. The move from there into the present station took place in the 1950s. The use of a horse-drawn fire engine came to an end in around 1926. The Aspatria Fire Brigade became part of the National Fire Service at the outset of the Second World War, part of the Cumberland Fire Service in 1947, and Cumbria Fire Service in 1974. It is manned by volunteer part-time fire-fighters to this day, who still turn out when the fire alarm sounds (albeit an electronic pager), to serve the town and surrounding area.

The Railway

'Speattry loup out' was the cry to third class passengers when the trains arrived at Aspatria; second class were told: 'Speattry change 'ere for Mealsyat'; while first class passengers were politely informed: 'Aspatriah, change heah for Mealsgate'. This connection with the Mealsgate branch has long since disappeared, although to this day you can still see the bay platform where the 'Baggra Bus' once waited. The branch train can be seen standing in the bay in one of the photographs. In fact the station of today bears little resemblance to the busy scenes of yesteryear. Some of the original buildings remain, but in a derelict state.

The Maryport and Carlisle Railway was initially opened from Maryport to Arkleby Pit on 15 July 1840, the remaining 1¾-mile extension to Aspatria being opened on 12 April 1841. The line from Carlisle to Wigton was built next to pacify the Carlisle shareholders and the gap remained between

Aspatria railway station showing 'Baggra Bus' (the train for Mealsgate) on the left

Aspatria station in 1894, with the West Cumberland Dairy on the right

Aspatria station in the 1950s, showing how the dairy has grown

Aspatria station in the 1890s, showing
Maryport and Carlisle Railway
locomotive No. 24, station staff and a
local policeman

Wigton and Aspatria until 3 May 1843. Passengers were carried across the gap by stage coach. The Mealsgate branch (known as the Bolton Loop) was opened on 2 April 1866. The station had a very busy goods yard: there were cattle pens (the new auction mart being nearby), warehouses, and loading bays for the stone from Mr Graves' works, much of which was conveyed to Glasgow for export. There was heavy coal and coke traffic – the coal to Maryport docks for export to Ireland and the coke to the iron and steel works of West Cumberland. After the West Cumberland Dairy Company opened next to the station, it used the railway for transporting bulk milk in tankers to the people of London. Produce from the Brayton Estate was sent down from Baggrow destined for the local markets. The passengers were well catered for. There were welcoming coal fires in the waiting rooms, porters to help with their heavy luggage, and the stationmaster always on hand: the hours he had to work were long, 7 a.m. until 10 p.m. The signalman had plenty of work to do with all the traffic; the original signal box still stands but the signal frame was replaced in 1942 with a second-hand one built at Horwich, Lancashire. In the early years the only access from one platform to the other was via Bower Bridge, where a set of steep steps led down from the road to the west end of the Carlisle platform – so passengers took a short cut and walked across the line. In 1889, after many accidents and near misses, the company stated its intention to build an underground passage to enable passengers to cross the railway in safety. However, the tunnel never materialized and it wasn't until the 1890s that the footbridge was erected. It continues to be used today. Over the years various improvements were carried out by the company, adding new waiting rooms, toilets and so on; the changes can be seen by comparing the photographs. The Solway Junction Railway connected with the Maryport and Carlisle at Brayton Junction, and carried West Cumberland iron ore across the Solway viaduct to the foundries of Lanarkshire.

The old West Cumberland Dairy is seen in the 1894 photograph, and its successor, the Milk Marketing Board cheese factory in the later picture. What a different scene today when the land on the Maryport platform side of the line is taken up by factories, the station area now has the look of neglect and it is an unmanned halt. It is almost certain that if Sir Wilfred Lawson, who was Chairman of the Maryport and Carlisle Railway Company from 1874 to 1906, could see it now, he would use the same words today as he used at one of the company board meetings: 'Sirs, we are going forwards – backwards!' How true.

CHAPTER SIX

The Town

The selection of photographs in this section need no explanation, giving views of the town from the turn of the century to the 1930s. The approaches to the town from east and west, and the town itself have changed very little over the last 100 years. Most of the fine Victorian public buildings have been well preserved.

The decision to name the streets and number the houses was taken by the Aspatria Urban District Council in July 1901. Until that date the east end was known as Newtown, Harriston Road as Mill Road, Queen Street and King Street were Main Street, Midtown and Front Street and North Road was Priests Lane.

The removal of the gas tanks made a great change to Lawson Street, as did the demolition of the brewery at the junction of Brayton Road and Lawson Street — although the area is still known as Brewery Corner. In 1883 Benjamin Kendall sold his brewery and it became Robert Bell's Central Aerated Water Works, probably because in 1884, according to the local paper, more people in the town were drinking mineral waters than alcohol.

The Noble Temple was erected in 1872 and used for a time as the infant school. Sunday lectures were held regularly, and 'H' Company, 5th Cumberland Battalion of the Border Regiment (Territorials) used it as a drill hall until their permanent quarters were built in the Outgang in 1914. In 1919 Mr Towers started his Temple Picture House here and there was much rivalry between this and Queen's Palace for audiences. Agricultural shows were held in the Noble Croft Field opposite the hall, where the council estate was built in 1937. The field was also used by the local cricket club.

Aspatria Board School's foundation stone was laid by Mr McTear on 5 March 1894 and the official opening was by Lady Lawson in 1895. The cost of the building was £4,776 13s 4d, which included the master's house, but the cost of school furniture was an extra £250. At the time girls, boys and infants were segregated. The school photo was taken in September 1921. While taking down a block of buildings at Millers Farm to build the access road to the school, part of an old house was found. It dated back to 1611, and had the initials FA carved over the door. The then farmhouse was built in 1696.

Mr Joseph Pattinson, owner of Pattinson's the Chemist, had a great interest in photography, and many of the pictures in this book were taken by him or his son Eric. Joseph began his career with Mr Sparks, who started his chemist shop at 43 Queen Street in 1894. Joseph took over the business about the turn of the century. He moved next to (Midtown) 48 King Street, the clock above the shop still being *in situ*. The move to the present premises at 56 King Street was made on completion of the new shop, which was built adjoining Springwell House. In the early 1930s Eric took over the business of Mr Litt at 61 Queen Street, and ran the two chemist shops until his retirement in 1957. The Queen Street shop was closed by the new owner, Mr R. Southgate, in 1960. A feature that many will remember was Pattinson's travelling chemist van, begun in 1934 and operated by the author's father, Andrew Douglas – Tom Routledge doing the honours during the war years. The van operated within a 10-mile radius of the town, and was greatly missed when taken off the road in 1948.

The photo of Sanderson's old shops in King Street was taken in 1901, before demolition in 1903. The new shop is easily recognized today. One of the greatest changes in the town was the demolition of the Waverley Hotel and its adjoining cottages in the late 1960s. St Kentigerns Way now stands on part of the site.

Aspatria Industrial Co-operative Society was formed in 1865, the original and present premises being at 32 King Street. The Society prospered and the premises grew, having in its heyday warehousing, butchery, a large stable block (eventually converted into a small bakery for the store), a large drapery and menswear department, boot and shoe department, and furniture store, along with a thriving coal business, milk round and two travelling shops. Many branches were opened in the area and much property was owned by the Society. Three houses were built for staff in 1880 next to the old fire station, which was eventually purchased and incorporated into the shops. The first of the houses, No. 34, was the first house in the town to have a supply of electricity, being connected to the Society's own generator. Only two of the houses now remain. A good 'divi' was always paid to its members twice yearly. In the 1970s, as was the case with many small Societies, Aspatria merged with Carlisle South End Co-op, and this in turn became part of the Cumbrian Society. All branches and departments were closed, leaving only the original premises.

The present Midland Bank premises were built in 1874 and was originally three businesses in one, the post office, the Cumberland Union Bank, and drapers and tailors. All departments were run by Mr Joseph Forrester. In 1890 Mr John Tyndale bought an old house next door to the Bank and converted it to two shops (now Bouch's). Castle Terrace with its fine houses, built in the

Interior of Pattinson's shop, 1898

Pattinson's chemist (Midtown), King Street,
early 1900s

The author's father, Andrew Douglas, with Pattinson's travelling chemist's van outside the shop at 61 Queen Street (formerly Litt's Chemists), 1934. (43 Queen Street had been closed by this time)

Joseph Pattinson's chemist shop, 43 Queen Street, 1898

1880s by Mr Graves, has lost the two pairs of steps that led down on to the road, and also the beautiful trees that once flourished there.

The Reading and Recreation Rooms are opposite Castle Terrace. Opened in 1894, the fine building housed a library, reading rooms, billiard hall and games room. It eventually became an ice cream parlour, craft shop, amusement arcade and is now a private dwelling.

The Queen's Palace Cinema was owned by Charles Over, and was known locally as 'Charlies'. In 1911 it was entirely lit by electricity from its own generator and many people enjoyed Biddall's shows there. Later it became known as the Palace Cinema, and is now a Bingo hall.

At the Market Square the old established firm of Bouch still trades, and the 'Bray Lamp', although moved from its original position in the middle of the junction, is still nearby.

Near the Brandraw Hotel there was an old inn, the Half Moon. It was bought by Mr Frear of the Station Hotel in 1891, who intended to make alterations to the old building before occupying it. Possibly the Brandraw Hotel itself is the original Half Moon site.

Aspatria Agricultural Co-operative Society was the first of its kind in Great Britain, starting in 1869 and bringing together a group of farmers. Henry Thompson, the veterinary surgeon, was its first secretary. In February 1920 the Society gave a dinner in the Public Hall, at which a presentation was made to Mr Thompson for his fifty years as secretary. He received a cheque for £500 and an inscribed silver salver.

The Market Square (known earlier as Brandraw Green) has itself been the scene of many celebrations, markets, fairs, strolling theatres and on a few occasions Bostock and Wombwell's Menagerie.

Aspatria Public Hall, also known as the Market Hall, was built in 1872 at a cost of £1,300. Mr H.A. Clarke of Prospect House was the first chairman and Mr Henry Thompson took over the role in 1887. The clock in the tower was made by Mr C. Stonehouse, watchmaker of Aspatria, cost £75 and was the gift of Mr J.W. Johnstone of Outgang who was one of the original promoters. The Hall was used for many College functions, public meetings, dancing, roller skating and was also licensed as a theatre. There was also a roller skating rink in the Waverley Hall.

There are still fine houses surrounding the Green. The Agricultural College building was converted from Beacon House, a tower being added to the centre of the original house and a new wing added to the east end.

At the top of West Street the pond once again flourishes, after being dug out and restored as a wildlife venture by the pupils of Beacon Hill school. Just off Outgang Road we find the War Memorial Park alongside St Mungo's Park housing estate, the land for the estate being purchased from Mr T. Ostle

Sanderson's old shop before demolition, 1901

Sanderson's new shop with brothers Tommy (on the left) and Willy (on the right)

Queen Street, looking west towards King Street

in February 1920. The Park boasted tennis courts, bowling green, putting green, children's playground, football pitch and flower gardens. A short Armistice service is held each November at the main entrance with its splendid gates in honour of the dead of two world wars.

Aspatria went through a great period of change between the 1870s and 1890s, with all the new public buildings, houses and shops going up and the demolition of old shops and thatched cottages. Even before these years many changes had taken place with the turnpike roads and the coming of the railway. Time doesn't stand still and the present time is making its own changes, which in turn will become part of history.

Lawson Street. The gas works was on the left

Lawson Street: the other end at Brayton Road/Brewery Corner

Victoria Park and Park Road, corner of Springkell

Primitive Methodist chapel, manse and cottages, Queen Street

Queen Street, looking east. Note the collier with a sack of coal on his bicycle frame, and the delivery vans. The brewery is in the distance

New Wesleyan chapel and Queen Street: compare with the photograph on p. 9 (top)

Jackson's Tailors, King Street, with Pattinson's on the left

King Street, looking towards Queen Street

King Street, looking towards Market Square, with Bob Bell up the lamp post. 'Lib' Sewell from Waverley Temperance Hotel is on the right with a child

Wintry scene in King Street at the turn of the century

The Aspatria Co-op staff can be seen outside the shop in 1901. From left to right they are: Skillicorn, Benson, Miles, Cameron, Reay, Young, Pattinson, Husbands, Lawson, Wood

The Co-op warehouse staff, mid-1920s. From left to right: Walter Faulder (engineer), George Walker (carter), Wilty Bell (grocer), Will Douglas (warehouseman and stableman – author's grandfather), Willy Holliday (carter)

Waverley Temperance Hotel. Left to right: Fearon Sewell (son), Frank Sewell and Elizabeth ('Lib') Sewell. The other man is unidentified.

Waverley Hotel and cottages, looking west towards Market Square

Castle Terrace, showing the steps down to the road

Castle Terrace, King Street, Stobbart's petrol pumps on the right

Reading and Recreation rooms on King Street

Tweddle's Sun Hotel, King Street

Mr Henry Thompson, veterinary surgeon (wearing panama hat) and his son Charles (on the right) standing outside their surgery/chemist and druggist shop, with the Bray gas lamp in its original position

Market Square, showing Grapes Hotel with third floor added. The Bray lamp now carries direction signs

Public Hall, Agricultural College and Monument, Market Square

Market Square looking towards West Street, with Brandraw House on the left

West Street, with Jackson's Pond

Council Terrace, built just after the First World War

The War Memorial Park entrance

Part of the recreation grounds in the Memorial Park

St Mungo's Park estate taken from the church tower

Station Road, looking towards the Market Square

CHAPTER SEVEN

Leisure and Special Occasions

Aspatria Collieries Silver Band was set up in the 1860s by Mr Harris, the owner of Brayton Domain Collieries, who lent the sum of £1,000 to his employees to purchase the silver instruments for a band. The money was paid back to Mr Harris, each miner paying 1*d* per week until the loan had been repaid. When the last of the pits closed the band became the Aspatria Town Band, and lasted until 1967. The instruments were then given to the Beacon Hill Secondary School for the use of the pupils.

In the early 1930s there were twenty-six members, nineteen of whom were colliers, and among them were five fathers and six of their sons. Townspeople will remember the band playing for the town carnivals, their annual appearance at the Remembrance services, and playing around the town on Christmas morning. Three of the bandsmen in the photographs are still alive today, namely Len Hewitson, Albert Mounsey and Jack Ashworth.

During its existence the band had four rehearsal rooms; they started in a room above the old fire station at the Auction Market, then moved to the Market Hall. After this they used the Waverley Hall behind the Temperance Hotel. Latterly they practised at the Social Centre behind Bedford Square. In 1947 a house to house collection throughout the town raised money to renovate the instruments.

As well as the Colliery Band, the Volunteer Fire Brigade had its own brass band and the 'Terriers' – 'H' Company, 5th Battalion, Border Regiment had a military band. The Salvation Army Band was a regular performer at religious gatherings in the town.

Aspatria Male Voice Choir was first formed by Mr James Cobb in 1894, but little is known about this choir or when it disbanded.

The choir was reformed on 20 November 1946 with eight members and Mrs J.B. Holliday as the conductor, and rehearsals were held in the Lawson Street Methodist Sunday School building. Len Hewitson was the assistant conductor, Mrs Arnott and Miss M. Goodall, the pianists. Mr R.F. Beattie, the local headmaster, was the president, S. Raine the chairman, J. Holliday the secretary and J. Stoddart the treasurer. Its first public appearance was at the Carlisle and District Musical Festival in the following year. Concerts were given in various places for churches and charities, and its signature tune was

'Bless This House'. By 1948 the choir had twenty-eight members, the youngest being seventeen and the oldest seventy-two.

Aspatria Townswomen's Guild Choir was also founded by Mrs J.B. Holliday, who conducted and trained them for many years. Mrs Elsie Arnott took over after Mrs Holliday's retirement. Mrs Arnott also formed, trained and conducted the Aspatria Songsters and the Ladies' Choir.

A children's concert in aid of the NSPCC was given at the Social Centre on 9 and 10 May 1950. It was arranged by Mrs Elsie Arnott, assisted by Irene Holliday, the pianist, and Millie Watson, the local organizer of the NSPCC. The Annie Robinson Dance Troupe from Maryport also took part. Electrical work was by Tinnion & Kyfin, and flowers came from Brayton Gardens. The concert was a great success, with all credit due to Mrs Arnott who had rehearsed the children to perfection. Over 600 tickets were sold for the two performances, and a considerable sum of money was raised.

The Wings for Victory Parade took place on 29 May 1943, and the photograph shows the procession going up King Street towards the Market Square, where a display of aircraft and military items had been arranged.

Aspatria School Canteen was officially opened on Tuesday 2 May 1950 by Gordon Bessey, Director of Education for Cumberland. He was assisted by a pupil, Barbara Wilkinson, whose birthday it was that day.

Cart trips were an annual summer event, the forerunner of bus and train excursions. They were organized by the various chapels and the church for the Sunday School pupils, usually to Silloth or Allonby. The horses and carts were loaned by local farmers and businesses. With the advent of the internal combustion engine the distances of these trips was increased, and the charabancs went as far as Keswick, a trip around the Lakes also being possible. Excursions were also made by train to Seascale and St Bees, the scholars being led to the railway station by the Fire Brigade Band, to join their specially chartered train. The local Co-op also had its own trip, as can be seen in one of the photographs.

Merrymaking in King Street, with the Reading Rooms on the right and Castle Terrace on the left

Carnival or May Queen Parade at the Market Square, Brandraw House in the background

Primitive Methodist Sunday School procession, with Mr Peter Yeowart on the left

Band of Hope passing the Primitive Methodist chapel at Tunnel Bridge Queen Street

The Boys Brigade with the Revd Mr Furmston in the centre of the front row

Cart trip outside Pattinson's chemist, King Street

Aspatria Fire Brigade Brass Band, 1905

Aspatria Colliery Silver Band, 1931. Back row, left to right: Len Hewitson, G. Robinson, J. Thompson, T. Ross, R. Stoddart, Albert Mounsey, J. Atkinson, J. Cuthell, T. Graves, G. Bell. Middle row: H. Graves, J.W. Glencross, W. Robinson, J. Ashworth, J. Pearson, J. Hewitson, W. Robinson, I. Maughan, J. Wilkinson, J.W. Harker, G. Benson. Front row: R. Tunstall, T. Hewitson, J.W. Atkinson, W. Atkinson, C. Thompson, T. Tunstall, G. Graham, J. Bell

Aspatria Town Band heading the carnival procession in the early 1950s, with Mr J.W. Atkinson (conductor) and Mr 'Willy' Hastings leading the band

Bowling match at the Harris Bowling Club, Harriston pit village.

Aspatria RU Football Club, Cumberland Cup winners 1911–12. Back row, left to right: Jack Bell, -?-, ? Walker, Reg Furmston, Dr W.F. Coulthard, Jim Furguson, Tom Storey, Reg Thompson, George Bell. Middle row: Dr John Robinson, Jim Beattie, 'Pudding' Graham, 'Gront' Holliday, 'Chick' Tweddle, John Walker, Alf Holliday. Front row: ? Graves

The Cumberland Rugby Cup winners celebrating their success outside the Station Hotel

Aspatria Co-operative staff outing. Back row, left to right: Jim Saul, -?-, Jim Scaife, George Walker, -?-, -?-. Second row: -?-, Jack Clark (shoemaker). Third row: centre is Effie Scaife, remainder not known. Front row: Cyril Graham on far right, others not known

Wings For Victory Parade in King Street, 29 May 1943

Aspatria Male Voice Choir, summer 1948. Back row, left to right: J. Pearson, Tony Wilkinson, Humphrey Berwick, Reg Baxter. Middle row: ? Glencross, Bill Murdoch, Jack Hodgson, J.B. Holliday, Len Hewitson, Harry Turner, Billy Tinnion, ? Hillary. Front row: Dan Stoddart, Jacky Stoddart, ? Ridley, 'Tucker' Bell, Renée Holliday, John Thompson, Joseph Holliday, Jo Holden, John Armstrong

Elsie Arnott's NSPCC Children's Concert Party, May 1950. Back row, left to right: Yvonne Wilkinson, Eileen Reay, Miriam Atkinson, Muriel Wetton, Alice Stoddart, Greta Carter, Frances Ridley. Front row: Valerie Little, Joyce Oliver, Elizabeth Brodie, Anne Douglas (your author), Mary Walker

Turn-of-the-century cart trip to Allonby

Elephants from Bostock and Wombwell's menagerie in King Street, on their visit to West Cumberland in 1929

Maths

Assessment Papers
Stretch

9-10 years

OXFORD

UNIVERSITY PRESS

UNIVERSITY PRESS

Great Clarendon Street, Oxford, OX2 6DP, United Kingdom

Oxford University Press is a department of the University of Oxford.
It furthers the University's objective of excellence in research, scholarship,
and education by publishing worldwide. Oxford is a registered trade mark of
Oxford University Press in the UK and in certain other countries

Text © Paul Broadbent 2015
Illustrations © Oxford University Press 2015

The moral rights of the authors have been asserted

First published in 2015

All rights reserved. No part of this publication may be reproduced,
stored in a retrieval system, or transmitted, in any form or by any
means, without the prior permission in writing of Oxford University
Press, or as expressly permitted by law, by licence or under terms
agreed with the appropriate reprographics rights organization.
Enquiries concerning reproduction outside the scope of the above
should be sent to the Rights Department, Oxford University Press, at
the address above.

You must not circulate this work in any other form and you must
impose this same condition on any acquirer

British Library Cataloguing in Publication Data
Data available

978-0-19-274210-0

10 9 8 7 6 5 4

Paper used in the production of this book is a natural, recyclable
product made from wood grown in sustainable forests.
The manufacturing process conforms to the environmental
regulations of the country of origin.

Printed in China

Acknowledgements

The publishers would like to thank the following for permissions to
use copyright material:

Page make-up: GreenGate Publishing Services, Tonbridge, Kent
Illustrations: GreenGate Publishing Services, Tonbridge, Kent
Cover illustrations: Lo Cole

Although we have made every effort to trace and contact all
copyright holders before publication this has not been possible in all
cases. If notified, the publisher will rectify any errors or omissions at
the earliest opportunity.

Links to third party websites are provided by Oxford in good faith
and for information only. Oxford disclaims any responsibility for
the materials contained in any third party website referenced in
this work.

Introduction

What is Bond?

The Bond *Stretch* titles are the most challenging of the Bond assessment papers, the number one series for the 11+, selective exams and general practice. Bond *Stretch* is carefully designed to challenge above and beyond the level provided in the regular Bond assessment range.

How does this book work?

The book contains two distinct sets of papers, along with full answers and a Progress Chart:

- Focus tests, accompanied by advice and directions, are focused on particular (and age-appropriate) maths question types encountered in the 11+ and other exams, but devised at a higher level than the standard *Assessment Papers*. Each Focus test is designed to help raise a child's skills in the question type as well as offer plenty of practice for the necessary techniques.

- Mixed papers are full-length tests containing a full range of maths question types. These are designed to provide rigorous practice for children working at a level higher than that required to pass the 11+ and other maths tests.

Full answers are provided for both types of test in the middle of the book.

Some questions may require a ruler or protractor. Calculators are not permitted.

How much time should the tests take?

The tests are for practice and to reinforce learning, and you may wish to test exam techniques and working to a set time limit. We would recommend your child spends 55 minutes answering the 50 questions in each Mixed paper.

You can reduce the suggested time by five minutes to practise working at speed.

Using the Progress Chart

The Progress Chart can be used to track Focus test and Mixed paper results over time to monitor how well your child is doing and identify any repeated problems in tackling the different question types.

Focus test 1   Place value

Tenths, hundredths and thousandths follow a decimal point, which is used to separate whole numbers from decimals.

Read these and write each number in figures.

1 seventy-eight thousand one hundred and three _____

2 six hundred thousand four hundred and eighty _____

3 Write the number that is 100 more than each of these.

19 909 → _____   93 990 → _____   60 901 → _____

4 What is £345.75 rounded to the nearest pound? _____

5 Write the numbers at each arrow.

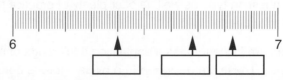

6   7

6 Complete these calculations.

$17.02 \times 100 =$ _____ $27.4 \times 100 =$ _____

7 Complete these calculations.

$3005 \div 100 =$ _____ $19 \div 100 =$ _____

8 Write these in order.   4.731   7.413   7.137   4.334

_____ < _____ < _____ < _____

9 Round each amount to the nearest whole number.

245.6 m → _____   853.91 ml → _____

10 Round each amount to the nearest tenth.

67.072 km → _____   391.745 kg → _____

11 Circle the smallest number and underline the largest number.

38.09   38.9   38.99   38.099   38.909

12 Mount Snowdon in Wales is 3560 feet in height. What is this rounded to the nearest 1000 feet? _____

Focus test 2 | Addition and subtraction

1 Join pairs of numbers that total 6.5

     2.9   1.6   5.8   2.6   4.9

         0.7   3.9   3.6

Write the missing numbers to complete these.

> Decide whether to work out the answer in your head, use rough notes or use a written method — and always check that your answer makes sense.

2
```
    □ 7 . 2 □
 +  4 □ . 4 7
 _____
    8 6 . 7 2
```

3
```
    2 8 . □ 6
 -  1 □ . 6 □
 _____
    1 0 . 7 7
```

4 Write the total weight of this group of parcels. _____

    | 9.45 kg | | 12.6 kg | | 13.07 kg |

5 A greenhouse costs £645.79. It costs an extra £87.54 to have it delivered and put up. What is the total cost? £ _____

6 Circle the two numbers with a difference of 2.7 and a total of 14.3

       9.3   8.7   3.9   8.5   7.6   5.8

Complete these calculations.

7
```
     8 3 6 9 7
   + 4 1 6 7 2
   _____
```

8
```
     5 0 0 6 8
   - 3 4 7 7 9
   _____
```

9 What is the missing number? $(17 - 8) +$ _____ $= 14$

10 Write in the missing digits 1, 2, 3, 4, 5 and 6.

   ___.9 + 3.___ = 10.3   5.___ + ___.9 = 7.1   ___.6 + ___.7 = 9.3

11 These are the bills for three meals at a café. What is the cost of each item?

| 1 sandwich
1 drink
Total: £3.70 | 1 drink
2 ice creams
Total: £3.10 |

| 2 ice creams
Total: £1.80 |

   1 sandwich = _____   1 drink = _____

   1 ice cream = _____

12 What are the numbers A and B?

   A = _____   B = _____

> A and B are two different whole numbers. A is 10 greater than B. A + B = 92

1 Complete this multiplication grid.

×	9		8
7		21	
	54		

> Remember: multiplication and division are inverse operations. Use this to help recall facts, for example:
>
> 3 x 6 = 18 and 6 x 3 = 18,
> so 18 ÷ 6 = 3 and 18 ÷ 3 = 6

2 Write the missing number. $7 \times 8 \times \underline{\qquad} = 560$

3 Complete this calculation.

$$
\begin{array}{r}
86 \\
\times\ 95 \\
\hline
 \\
\end{array}
$$

4 What is 2859 divided by 14?

$$14\overline{)2\,8\,5\,9}\quad \text{r}\underline{\qquad}$$

5 A ball of string is 48 m in length. What length of string will there be in 20 balls? _____

6 This is a 'divide by 40' machine. Write the missing numbers in the chart.

IN → | ÷ 40 | → OUT

IN	160	____	440	____	360
OUT	____	5	____	20	____

7 Plums are sold in boxes of 12. How many complete boxes can be filled from a bag of 80 plums? _____

8 Fence panels are 1.5 m wide. The perimeter of a garden is 45 m. How many panels are needed to put a fence around the garden? ____

9 Which number between 80 and 90 has a remainder of 5 when it is divided by 9? _____

10 Complete this.

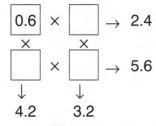

$$0.6 \times \boxed{} \to 2.4$$

11 Complete these, writing in the correct signs, =, < or >.

$$17 \times 8 \underline{\qquad} 16 \times 9$$
$$135 \div 5 \underline{\qquad} 132 \div 4$$

12 Which number, when multiplied by 30, gives the same answer as 45 × 12? _____

Multiples, factors and prime numbers

1 Circle the numbers that are multiples of 6.

72   92   114   87   69   99   106   80   96

2 Use each of these digits once to make a total that is a multiple of 5.

2   9   7   6   ☐☐ + ☐☐

3 20 is a common multiple of 4 and 5. Which of these numbers is also a common multiple of 4 and 5? Circle the correct answer.

9   16   60   30   45

4 What is the smallest number that is a common multiple of 4 and 6? _____

5 Circle the numbers that are **not** factors of 60.

1   2   3   4   5   6   7   8   9

6 Write the missing factors for 72.

(1, ____) (2, ____) (3, ____) (4, ____) (6, ____) (8, ____)

7 Write the factors of 36 in order, starting with 1.

36 → 1 ____ ____ ____ ____ ____ ____ ____ ____

8 Write these numbers in the correct part of the Venn diagram.

| 9 | 15 | 6 | 12 | 2 |
| 10 | 20 | 36 | | |

Multiple of 3 ⬭⬭ Factor of 18

9 What is the next prime number after the number 7? _____

Choose **two** of these digit cards each time to make 2-digit numbers.

10 A factor of 60 → ___ ___

11 A multiple of 9 → ___ ___

12 A prime number → ___ ___

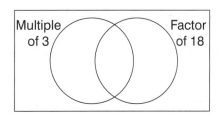
5   4   7   1

> A prime number only has two factors, 1 and itself. For example, 13 is a prime number as it can only be divided exactly by 1 and 13.

Fractions, decimals and percentages

1 Answer these.

$\frac{4}{5} + \frac{7}{10} = \square \frac{\square}{\square}$ $\frac{1}{2} - \frac{1}{3} = \frac{\square}{\square}$

2 Write the missing percentage or decimal to complete this table.

0.3	0.70	0.95	0.05	0.08
30%	70%	95%	5%	8%

3 Circle the fraction that is the same as the decimal number.

0.2 $\frac{1}{5}$ $\frac{1}{4}$ $\frac{1}{2}$ $\frac{3}{4}$

4 Join each improper fraction to the mixed number with the same value.

$\frac{7}{3}$ $\frac{7}{5}$ $\frac{13}{5}$ $\frac{5}{3}$

$1\frac{2}{5}$ $2\frac{3}{5}$ $1\frac{2}{3}$ $2\frac{1}{3}$

5 What is $\frac{3}{8}$ of 48? _____

6 Write < , > or = between each pair of fractions.

$\frac{2}{5}$ _____ $\frac{1}{4}$ $\frac{1}{2}$ _____ $\frac{7}{10}$ $\frac{3}{4}$ _____ $\frac{2}{3}$

Write the following fractions as percentages.

7 $\frac{7}{10}$ = _____   **8** $\frac{2}{5}$ = _____   **9** $\frac{3}{4}$ = _____

10 Change these test scores to percentages.

8 out of 10 →   _____%

16 out of 20 →   _____%

8 out of 25 →   _____%

> To change fractions to percentages find an equivalent fraction with the denominator 100.
>
> $\frac{3}{5}$ is equivalent to $\frac{60}{100}$
>
> $\frac{3}{5}$ = 60%

11 Circle the two cards that show less than $\frac{1}{2}$

$\frac{5}{7}$ 5%   .52 $\frac{2}{5}$ 0.7   52%

12 Look at this circle.

What fraction of this circle is shaded? _____

What percentage of this circle is shaded? _____

You can often find the pattern or rule in a sequence by looking at the difference between the numbers.

1 What is the next number in this sequence?

137 . 133   129   125   _____

2 What is the missing number in this sequence? Circle the correct answer.

121   100   _____   64   49   36   25

a 85   b 76   c 81   d 90

Write the missing numbers in these sequences.

3 _____   179   190   201   _____   223

4 6.5   _____   _____   11   12.5   14

5 6540   6450   _____   6270   6180   _____

6 In this sequence each number is half the previous number.

_____   _____   176   88   44   _____   _____

7 In this sequence each number is double the previous number.

_____   _____   10   20   40   _____   _____

8 What is the rule or pattern for this sequence? Circle the correct answer.

8279 8079 7879 7679   a − 20 b − 200 c − 2000 d − 2

9 What is the next square number in this sequence?

64   81   100   _____

10 Write the next number in this sequence.

1   3   6   10   _____

11 Describe the rule or pattern in the sequence above.

_____

12 Write the missing numbers in this sequence.

630   _____   642   _____   654

Look at these shapes.

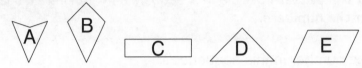

1 Which two shapes have no right angles? Shapes _____ and _____

2 What is the name of shape E? _____

3 Which shape has no lines of symmetry? _____

4 Which shape is not a quadrilateral? _____

5 Tick to show whether each angle is acute, obtuse, reflex or right-angled.

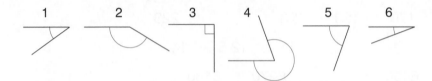

Angle	1	2	3	4	5	6
Acute						
Obtuse						
Reflex						
Right-angled						

6 Count the edges, faces and vertices on each shape and complete the chart.

Shape	Name	Faces	Edges	Vertices
	Square-based pyramid	_____	_____	_____
	Tetrahedron	_____	_____	_____
	Cuboid	_____	_____	_____
	Triangular prism	_____	_____	_____

The net of a solid or 3-D shape is what it looks like when it is opened out flat.

Name each of these shapes from the nets.

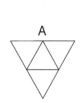

A

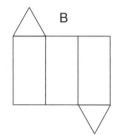

B

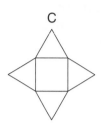

C

7 A _____

8 B _____

_____

9 C _____

_____

10 Draw a reflection of this shape. Use a ruler.

11 Measure angle A accurately. Use a protractor.

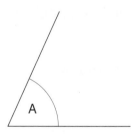

A

_____ °

12 Write the size of the missing angle for each shape.
Do not use a protractor.

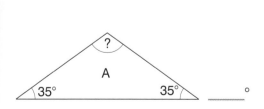

?

A

35°   35°   _____ °

60°

B

?

30°   _____ °

Focus test 8 — Area and perimeter

Area is usually measured in square centimetres or square metres, written as cm^2 and m^2. Always remember to write this at the end of the measurement.

Calculate the area and perimeter of these rectangles.

1

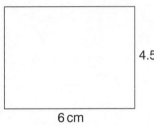

4.5 cm

Area = _____

Perimeter = _____

2

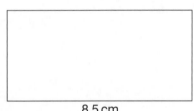

4 cm

Area = _____

Perimeter = _____

8.5 cm

3 What is the perimeter of a rectangular swimming pool, fifteen metres long and six metres wide? _____

Calculate the area of the shapes on this 1cm square grid.

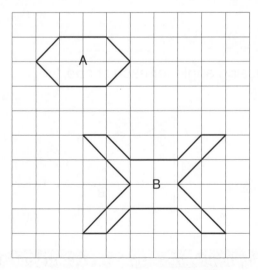

4 Shape A = _____ cm²   **5** Shape B = _____ cm²

6 What is the area of a square tile with a 20 cm side? _____

7 The area of a rectangle is 36 cm². One of the sides is 4 cm. What is the perimeter of the rectangle? _____

8 The perimeter of a rectangle is 24 cm. The length is double the width. What is the area of this rectangle?

Area = _____ cm²

Calculate the area of these shaded shapes.

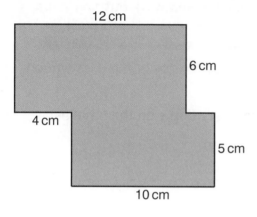

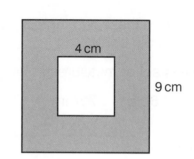

9 Area = _____ cm²

10 Area = _____ cm²

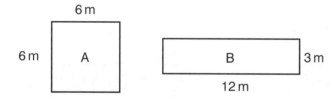

11 Which has the larger area? Underline the statement that is true.

A has the larger area   B has the larger area

The areas of A and B are the same.

12 Which has the longer perimeter, Shape A or Shape B? _____

Focus test 9 — Measures

1 What is the difference between the amount of liquid in these two jugs?

_____

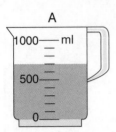

A

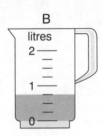

B

> Read scales carefully when measuring – look at the numbers written on the scales and work out the value of each unnumbered mark.

2 The liquid in these two jugs is poured into an empty bottle. How much liquid is in the bottle? _____

3 Write this set of measures in length order, starting with the smallest.

7.6 cm   70 mm   7.2 m   78 cm   0.75 m

_____   _____   _____   _____   _____

Smallest →

4 Sam is baking some cakes. He puts some flour on the scales and then adds some butter.

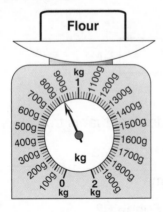

Flour

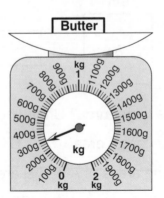

Butter

The weight of the flour is _____ g.

The weight of the butter is _____ g.

The total weight of the flour and butter is _____ kg _____ g.

5 A bus should arrive at 10:55 am but it is 12 minutes late. What time does the bus arrive?

_____

6 Write the missing times on this train timetable. Each train starts in Arden and takes the same amount of time to travel between each station.

Arden	09:50	11:28	_____
Blythe	_____	11:46	13:25
Chorton	10:34	_____	13:51
Dunley	10:52	_____	_____

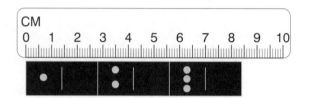

7 What is the total length of three dominoes? _____ cm

8 What is the total length of five dominoes? _____ cm

9 What is the difference in temperature between this pair of thermometers?

 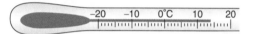

_____ °C

10 Each of these boxes is a different weight.

Boxes A and B weigh 14 kg altogether.

Box C weighs 4 kg more than Box A.

Boxes A and C weigh 16 kg altogether.

What is the weight of each box?

Box A _____

Box B _____

Box C _____

11 Calculate this division. Give your answer in the unit of measurement shown.

1.56 litres ÷ 6 = _____ ml

12 Write < or > to make this sentence true.

63 mm _____ 3.6 cm _____ 3.06 m _____ 360 cm _____ 36 mm

Now go to the Progress Chart to record your score!   Total   12

15

Transformations and coordinates

These show three types of transformation of shape A:

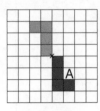

Rotation

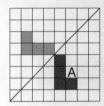

Reflection

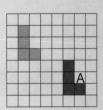

Translation

Write the correct transformation, **rotation**, **reflection** or **translation** for each of these.

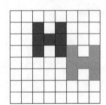

1 _____

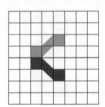

2 _____

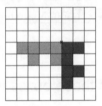

3 _____

4 Reflect the first tile in the tile next to it and below it. Continue the pattern to complete the whole grid.

(4, 1), (4, 6) and (0, 1) are the three vertices of a right-angled triangle.

5 (4,1) is already marked on this grid. Plot the other two points and draw the triangle.

6 Circle the coordinates that are enclosed by the sides of the triangle.

(2, 2)   (3, 3)   (2, 4)

(1, 3)   (2, 3)   (3, 4)

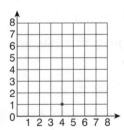

7 A, B and C are three vertices of a parallelogram. What are the coordinates of the fourth vertex, D? _____

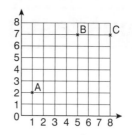

8 The parallelogram is translated to a new position on the grid. Vertex A is moved from (1, 2) to (0, 0). What are the new coordinates of the other three vertices?

B → _____ C → _____ D → _____

9 What are the missing coordinates for this square? (_____, _____)

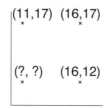

(11,17) (16,17)

(?, ?) (16,12)

10 Mark coordinate (−4, 2) on the grid. This is the fourth vertex of a quadrilateral. Draw two lines to complete this shape.

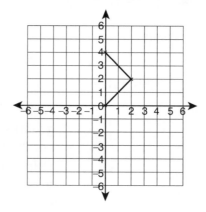

11 Coordinates (−1, 2) and (1, 2) are both on the line of symmetry of this shape.

True or False? _____

12 The shape is rotated anticlockwise around point (2, 2) so that the vertex at (−4, 2) is now at (2, −4). Where is the new position of the vertex at (0, 0)? _____

Charts, graphs and tables

This chart shows the height and shoe size for each child in a class.

1 How many children are taller than 149 cm? _____

2 How many children wear a shoe smaller than size 5? _____

3 How many children wear size 4 shoes and are shorter than 140 cm? _____

4 How many children are taller than 129 cm and wear a shoe size more than 4? _____

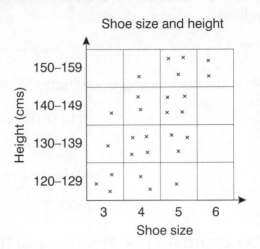

Shoe size and height

This graph shows the time and distance of a bus route.

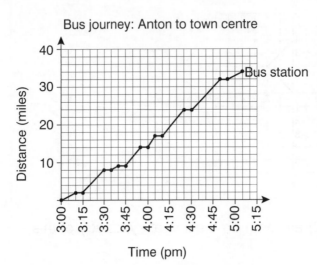

A distance–time line graph like this is continuous, so every point on the line has a value.

5 How many minutes in total is the bus at bus stops during the journey?

_____

6 How many miles does the bus travel between 3:30 and 3:45?

_____

7 How many miles in total does the bus travel? _____

8 This timetable shows the times the bus leaves each bus stop.

Use the graph to complete the two missing times.

Name of bus stop	Time bus departs
Anton	3:00pm
Bodham	3:15pm
Canby	_____pm
Duffield	3:45pm
Edgemore	4:00pm
Fenwell	4:10pm
Greatley	4:30pm
Heathend	_____pm
Town centre arrival time	5:05pm

In a science lesson a class measured the length of a shadow every 30 minutes and recorded the results on this graph.

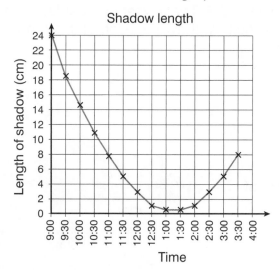

9 What length was the shadow at its shortest? _____

10 At approximately what time was the shadow 21 cm in length? _____

11 Circle the time period in which the shadow length decreased most quickly.

9:00–9:30   9:30–10:00   10:00–10:30

12 By how many centimetres did the shadow increase in length between 2 o'clock and 3 o'clock? _____

Now go to the Progress Chart to record your score!   Total   12

19

Mean, median, mode and probability

> Remember: to find the mean average add together all the scores and then divide that total by the number of scores you have used. The mean of 3, 5, 7 and 9 is 6.
>
> 3 + 5 + 7 + 9 = 24, divided by 4 is 6.

Look at this set of numbers.

(13) (29) (18) (21) (29)

1 The mean average is _____

2 The median is _____

3 The mode is _____

4 The mean of six numbers is 3.5. The lowest number is 2, the range is 5 and the modes are 2 and 3, with two of each of these numbers.

What are the six numbers? _____ _____ _____ _____ _____ _____

Look at the group of coins.

5 What coin value is the mode?

_____

6 What is the mean value of the coins? _____

7 Which coin value is the median? _____

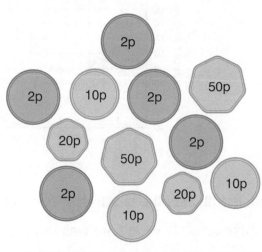

These are the weights of six parcels.

8 What is the mean weight?

_____

9 What is the mode?

_____

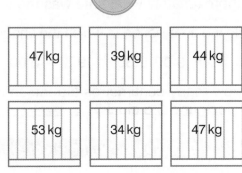

20

10 Write colours on this spinner so that you are equally likely to spin the colour blue as you are to spin green.

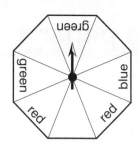

11 Spinner A has the numbers 1–5 and Spinner B has the numbers 1–6.

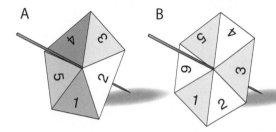

Circle the chance of spinning an odd number on Spinner A.

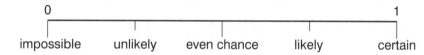

Circle the chance of spinning a 6 on Spinner A.

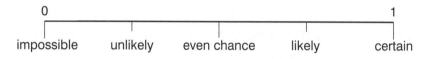

Circle the chance of spinning an odd number on Spinner B.

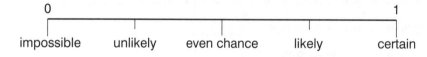

Circle the chance of spinning a multiple of 3 on Spinner B.

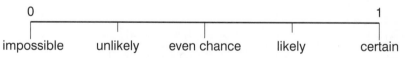

12 What is the likelihood of rolling a 7 on a 1–6 dice?

impossible   poor chance   even chance

good chance   certain

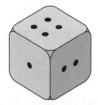

Mixed paper 1

Circle the digit in each number that represents the number written in words.

1 222222 two thousand

2 666666 six hundred thousand

3 111111 one hundred

4 444444 forty thousand

4

5–8 Write the missing numbers on this addition grid.

+	56	74
29		
	132	

4

Complete these, writing in the correct signs, =, < or >.

9 7 × 4 _____ 3 × 9

10 6 × 6 _____ 9 × 4

11 49 ÷ 7 _____ 48 ÷ 6

12 56 ÷ 8 _____ 54 ÷ 9

13 Divide 455 by 35.

5

Use these numbers to answer each question. | 25   26   27   28   29 |

14 Which number is a multiple of 3? _____

15 Which number is a common multiple of both 2 and 7? _____

16 Which number is a prime number? _____

17 Which number is a factor of 84? _____

4

Answer these.

18 $\frac{2}{3} + \frac{5}{6} = \boxed{}\frac{\boxed{}}{\boxed{}}$

19 $\frac{3}{4} + \frac{3}{10} = \boxed{}\frac{\boxed{}}{\boxed{}}$

2

Write these decimals as percentages.

20 0.7 = _____%

21 0.15 = _____%

2

Write the next number in each sequence.

22 0.2   1.7   3.2   4.7   _____

23 8490   8390   8290   8190   _____

24 81   64   49   36   _____

25 Write the missing number in this sequence.

15   30   60   _____   240   480   960

26–29 Complete the chart.

Shape name	Number of vertices	Number of edges
Pentagonal-based pyramid	_____	_____
Hexagonal prism	_____	_____

30–31 Calculate the area and perimeter of this rectangle.

6 cm

3.5 cm

Area =   _____ cm²

Perimeter = _____ cm

32 A square table has an area of 4 m². What is the length of one side of this table? _____ m

33 A shop wants to put flashing lights all the way round a window. The window is 120 cm wide by 325 cm high. Circle the length of lights that is the exact length to go the whole way round the window.

a 890 cm   **b** 900 cm   **c** 880 cm   **d** 980 cm

34 A cake is put in the oven at this time and needs to cook for 15 minutes. What time is the cake ready to take out of the oven? _____

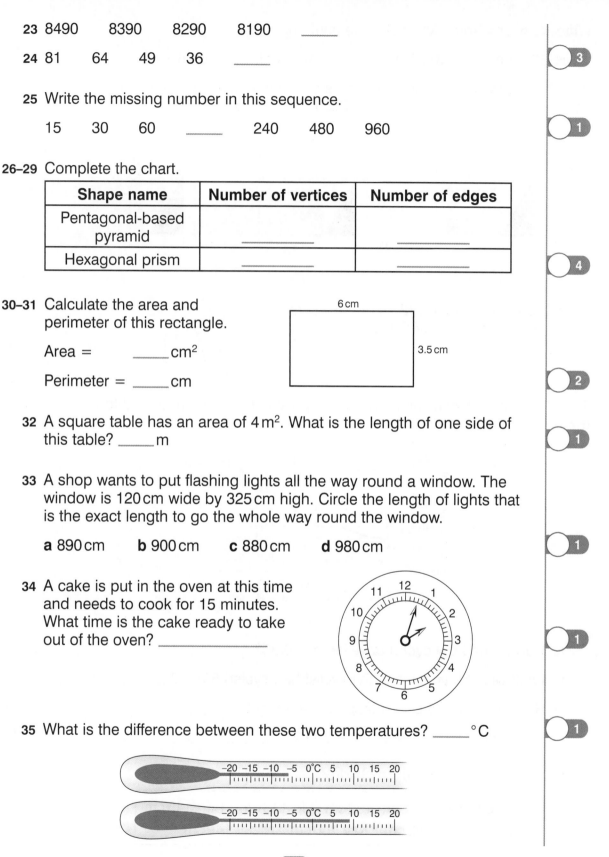

35 What is the difference between these two temperatures? _____ °C

-20 -15 -10 -5 0°C 5   10   15   20

-20 -15 -10 -5 0°C 5   10   15   20

23

Write <, > or = to make each statement true.

36 33.3 km _____ 3330 m   **37** 60 ml _____ 0.06 litres

Write the word that describes the transformation of the triangle in each question. Choose from **rotation**, **reflection** or **translation**.

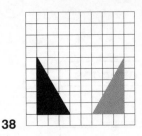   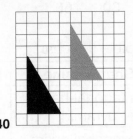

38 _____   **39** _____   **40** _____

41 Coordinates (1, 0), (2, 3) and (6, 3) are all on this line. True or False?

_____

These are the distances and times of a cyclist in the London to Brighton cycle race.

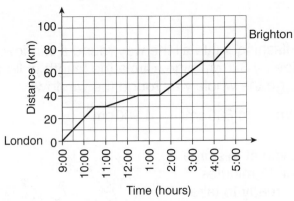

42 How far had the cyclist travelled by 10:30? _____

43 What was the time when the cyclist had cycled 55 km? _____

44 How long did the cyclist stop to rest altogether? _____

45 How far did the cyclist travel in total? _____

These are the heights of seven children.

Lee 157 cm   Sam 152 cm   Jo 148 cm   Ben 145 cm
Eve 152 cm   Kay 150 cm   Nicky 149 cm

24

46 Which is the median height? _____

47 Which height is the mode? _____

48 What is the mean average height, rounded to the nearest whole
centimetre? _____ ⟩ 3

Choose one of these words to answer the questions.

┌───┐
│   impossible   poor chance   even chance   │
│   good chance   certain   │
└───┘

49 What is the chance of throwing a 6 on a dice? _____

50 What is the chance that the sun will set in London today? _____ ⟩ 2

Now go to the Progress Chart to record your score!   Total ⟩ 50

Mixed paper 2

Write the number that is 100 more than each of these.

1 77 945 → _____   **2** 50 982 → _____

3 16 900 → _____   **4** 38 199 → _____ ⟩ 4

5 Write the number shown on this abacus.

_____ ⟩ 1

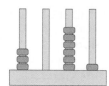

Complete these calculations.

6
```
    58471
  + 35637
  _____

  _____
```

7
```
    50028
  − 34779
  _____

  _____
```
⟩ 2

8 Increase 4.5 by 2.6 _____

9 What is 7.3 take away 1.8? _____ ⟩ 2

10 What number when divided by 12 has an answer of 4 remainder 5?

_____

11 Which number, when multiplied by 40, gives the same answer as 8 × 30? _____

2

Underline the correct answer.

12 0.3 × 9 =   0.027   0.27   2.7   2.07   27

13 0.8 × 4 =   2.8   3.6   0.32   0.36   3.2

2

14–19 Write these numbers in the correct part of the Venn diagram.

6	8	10
12	14	16

6

Circle the fraction that is the same as the decimal number.

20 0.8 $\frac{1}{8}$ $\frac{3}{4}$ $\frac{4}{5}$ $\frac{2}{3}$ $\frac{5}{8}$

21 6.75 $6\frac{5}{7}$ $3\frac{1}{4}$ $7\frac{5}{6}$ $6\frac{3}{4}$ $6\frac{4}{5}$

2

Write <, > or = between each pair of fractions.

22 $\frac{2}{5}$ _____ $\frac{5}{15}$ **23** $\frac{3}{4}$ _____ $\frac{9}{12}$

2

Write the missing numbers in each sequence.

24–25 463 _____ 459 _____ 455

26–27 88 _____ 100 _____ 112

4

Write the name of the shape described in each question. Choose from this list:

Rectangle   Tetrahedron   Cylinder   Regular hexagon

Sphere   Rhombus   Triangular prism

28 Name the flat shape that has 6 equal length sides and 6 lines of symmetry. _____

29 Name the 2-D shape that has 4 right angles, 2 pairs of different length sides and 2 lines of symmetry. _____

Any answer that requires units of measurement should be marked wrong if the correct units have not been included.

Focus test 1

1 78 103
2 600 480
3 20 009, 94 090, 61 001
4 £346
5 6.4, 6.68, 6.83
6 1702, 2740
7 30.05, 0.19
8 4.334 < 4.731 < 7.137 < 7.413
9 246 m, 854 ml
10 67.1 km, 391.7 kg
11 (38.09), 38.99
12 4000 feet

Focus test 2

1 (2.9, 3.6) (1.6, 4.9) (5.8, 0.7) (2.6, 3.9)

2
```
   37.25
 + 49.47
   86.72
```
(bold digits: **37**.**25**, **49**.47)

3
```
   28.46
 − 17.69
   10.77
```
(bold digits: 28.**46**, −**17**.**69**)

4 35.12 kg
5 £733.33
6 8.5, 5.8
7 125 369
8 15 289
9 5
10 **6**.9 + 3.**4**, 5.**2** + **1**.9, **3**.6 + **5**.7 *or* **5**.6 + **3**.7
11 £2.40, £1.30, 90p
12 51, 41

Focus test 3

1

×	9	3	8
7	**63**	21	**56**
6	54	**18**	**48**

2 10
3 8170
4 204 r 3
5 960 m
6

IN	160	**200**	440	**800**	360
OUT	**4**	5	**11**	20	**9**

7 6
8 30
9 86
10

0.6 × **4** → 2.4
× ×
7 × **0.8** → 5.6
↓ ↓
4.2 3.2

11 <, <
12 18

Focus test 4

1 72, 114, 96
2 79 + 26, *or* 29 + 76
3 60
4 12
5 7, 8, 9
6 72, 36, 24, 18, 12, 9
7 36 → 2, 3, 4, 6, 9, 12, 18, 36
8

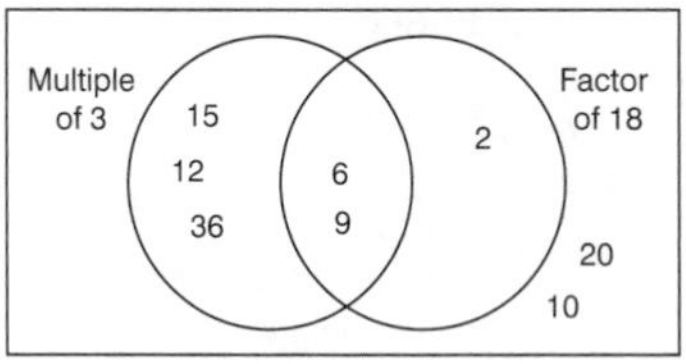

9 11
10 1 and 5
11 5 and 4, *or* 4 and 5
12 Any of: 1 and 7, *or* 7 and 1, *or* 4 and 7, *or* 4 and 1

Focus test 5

1 $1\frac{1}{2}$ and $\frac{1}{6}$
2

0.3	**0.7**	0.95	**0.05**	0.08
30%	70%	**95%**	5%	**8%**

3 $\frac{1}{5}$
4 $\frac{7}{3}$ and $2\frac{1}{3}$, $\frac{7}{5}$ and $1\frac{2}{5}$, $\frac{13}{5}$ and $2\frac{3}{5}$, $\frac{5}{3}$ and $1\frac{2}{3}$
5 18
6 >, <, >
7 70%
8 40%
9 75%
10 80%, 80%, 32%
11 5%, $\frac{2}{5}$
12 $\frac{4}{10}$ *or* $\frac{2}{5}$, 40%

Focus test 6

1 121
2 c
3 168, 212
4 8, 9.5
5 6360, 6090
6 704, 352, 22, 11
7 2.5, 5, 80, 160
8 b
9 121
10 15
11 Adding consecutive numbers: +2, +3, +4, +5
12 636, 648

Focus test 7

1 A and E
2 Parallelogram
3 E
4 D
5 1. acute; 2. obtuse; 3. right-angled; 4. reflex; 5. acute; 6. acute
6 5, 8, 5; 4, 6, 4; 6, 12, 8; 5, 9, 6
7 Tetrahedron
8 Triangular prism
9 Square-based pyramid
10

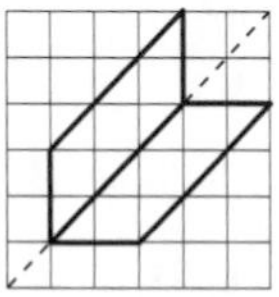

11 65°
12 110°, 90°

Focus test 8

1 27 cm^2, 21 cm
2 34 cm^2, 25 cm
3 42 m
4 6 cm^2
5 10 cm^2
6 400 cm^2
7 26 cm
8 32 cm^2
9 122 cm^2
10 65 cm^2
11 The areas of A and B are the same.
12 B

Focus test 9

1 50 ml
2 1450 ml
3 70 mm, 7.6 cm, 0.75 m, 78 cm, 7.2 m
4 850 g, 300 g, 1 kg 150 g
5 11:07am
6

Arden	09:50	11:28	**13:07**
Blythe	**10:08**	11:46	13:25
Chorton	10:34	**12:12**	13:51
Dunley	10:52	**12:30**	**14:09**

ANSWERS

7 8.4 cm
8 14 cm
9 23 °C
10 6 kg, 8 kg, 10 kg
11 260 ml
12 63 mm > 3.6 cm < 3.06 m < 360 cm > 36 mm

Focus test 10

1 translation
2 reflection
3 rotation
4

5
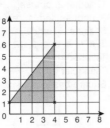

6 (2, 2), (2, 3), (3, 3), (3, 4)
7 (4, 2)
8 (4, 5), (7, 5), (3, 0)
9 (11, 12)
10
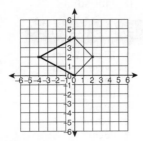

11 True
12 (4, 0)

Focus test 11

1 6
2 14
3 6
4 12
5 35 minutes
6 1 mile
7 34 miles
8 3:35pm, 4:55pm
9 0.5 cm or $\frac{1}{2}$ cm
10 9:15am
11 9:00–9:30
12 4 cm

Focus test 12

1 22
2 21
3 29
4 2, 2, 3, 3, 4, 7
5 2p
6 15p
7 10p
8 44 kg
9 47 kg
10 3 blue, 3 green, 2 red *or* 2 blue, 2 green, 4 red
11 likely, impossible, even chance, unlikely
12 impossible

Mixed paper 1

1 22②222
2 ⑥66666
3 111①11
4 4④4444

5–8

+	56	74
29	**85**	**103**
76	132	**150**

9 >
10 =
11 <
12 >
13 13
14 27
15 28
16 29
17 28
18 $1\frac{1}{2}$
19 $1\frac{1}{20}$
20 70%
21 15%
22 6.2
23 8090
24 25
25 120

26–29

Shape name	Number of vertices	Number of edges
Pentagonal-based pyramid	6	10
Hexagonal prism	12	18

30 21 cm²
31 19 cm
32 2 m
33 a 890 cm
34 2:18
35 15 °C
36 >

37 =
38 reflection
39 rotation
40 translation
41 False
42 30 km
43 2:30
44 2 hours
45 90 km
46 150 cm
47 152 cm
48 150 cm
49 poor chance
50 certain

Mixed paper 2

1 78 045
2 51 082
3 17 000
4 38 299
5 3061
6 94 108
7 15 249
8 7.1
9 5.5
10 53
11 6
12 2.7
13 3.2

14–19
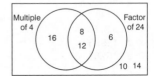

20 $\frac{4}{5}$
21 $6\frac{3}{4}$
22 >
23 =
24 461
25 457
26 94
27 106
28 Regular hexagon
29 Rectangle
30 Tetrahedron
31 Cylinder
32 75 m²
33 35 m
34 8 cm
35 4 cm
36 A
37 80.25 kg
38 750 g
39 C
40 C
41 (−2, 5)

42

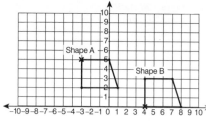

43 130
44 40
45 350
46 true
47 16
48 15
49 14
50 5

Mixed paper 3

1 4000
2 3000
3 4000
4 4000
5 2000
6–7 2.9 and 5.4
8–9 3.6 and 5.4
10–13

IN	150	**240**	360	450	**600**
OUT	**5**	8	**12**	15	20

14–15 29 and 59
16 112
17 12
18 90%
19 60%
20 $\frac{1}{4}$
21 $\frac{3}{4}$
22 b 83
23 d 2.5
24 3530
25 3630
26 Cuboid
27 55°
28 D
29–30

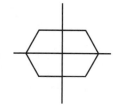

31 7 cm
32 3 cm
33 38 m
34 84 m²
35 2600 ml
36 1750 ml
37 850 ml
38 4.35 litres

39–40

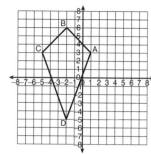

41 Translation
42 (0, 5)
43 2
44 141 cm–150 cm
45 8
46 25
47 even chance
48 unlikely
49 likely
50 impossible

Mixed paper 4

1–4 4.06, 4.55, 5.4, 5.82
5 83.08
6 31.71
7 2918 km
8 4098 km
9 6
10 5760
11 6
12 119
13–14 56 and 91
15–16 (3, 18)
17 $3\frac{1}{2}$
18 $2\frac{2}{5}$
19 20
20 12
21–22 56, 3.5
23–24 683, 708
25 66°
26 sometimes
27 120°
28 11 cm²
29 8 cm²
30 Room A
31 The perimeters of Room A and
B are the same length.
32–35 2.8 cm, 82 mm, 0.28 m, 82 cm
36–39

40 Kite
41 1
42 acute
43 600 grams
44 15 ounces
45–46 150 grams, 300 grams
47 44 kg
48 40 kg
49 42 kg
50 39 kg

Mixed paper 5

1 6
2 2310
3 18.06
4 0.72
5 6433
6 40.54
7 42 630
8 70 275
9 33 r 13
10 8 kg
11–12 3 and 23
13 126
14 4
15 17
16–17 3, 19
18 23.4
19 17.7
20 $\frac{14}{3}$
21 $\frac{19}{8}$
22 92
23 101
24 379
25 376
26 3
27 2
28 1
29 3
30 10 cm
31 57 m²
32 31 m
33 320 m
34–35 12:07, 13:03 (or 1:03 pm)
36 1 hour 13 minutes
37 12:35
38–39 A →(−6, 1) B→ (−6, 4)
40 (−5, 3)
41 (−2, 8)
42 4
43 7
44 4
45 18
46 even chance
47 35 cm
48 25 cm
49 20 cm
50 20.5

ANSWERS

Mixed paper 6

1 34.064
2 36.604
3 19.159
4 19.581
5 £47.54
6 £317.39
7 £42.49
8 £5.05
9 26 cm
10 84 years
11 7200 km
12 255
13–16

24	48
36	60

17–18 0.2, $\frac{1}{5}$
19–20 $\frac{7}{8}$, $\frac{1}{2}$
21 2199
22 7.6
23 510
24 c –900
25 142°
26 85°
27 65°
28 135°
29 144°
30 30.4 cm²
31 23.6 cm
32 140 m²
33 80 m
34 625.5 ml
35 50 ml
36 4300 g
37 900 g
38 340 g
39–42 (3, 0) (0, 7) (7, 4) (4, 3)
43 240
44 June
45 100
46 August
47 poor chance
48 good chance
49 impossible
50 5

Mixed paper 7

1 £187.30
2 £31.00
3 £15
4 £25
5–6 8.6, 9.4
7 1.7
8 18.3
9 911 r5 or 911.6
10 536 r4 or 536.6
11 37
12 5 × 11 × 13

13 45°
14–15 96, 128
16–17 (2, 46)
18 25%
19 $\frac{1}{3}$
20 <
21 60%
22 d 140
23–24 49, 81
25 21
26–29

D	C
A	B

30 96 m²
31 354 m²
32 60 fence panels
33

34 9 cm
35 22.5 cm
36 8 kg
37 4 kg
38 3 kg
39

40 (6, 7)
41

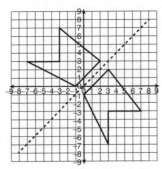

42 (3, –3)
43 £1
44 £1.50
45 50 p
46 £3
47 7
48 16
49 0.6
50 50%

Mixed paper 8

1–4 4.602 < 4.604 < 6.024 < 6.246
5 Eight thousand and one
6 Three thousand and twenty
7 8
8 27
9–10 1.8 kg, 2.8 kg
11 69
12 6
13 63
14 12
15 False
16 True
17 False
18 True
19–20 0.8, $\frac{3}{5}$
21 0.4
22 0.07
23 $\frac{4}{5}$
24 80%
25 10.0
26 a halve the number
27–28 1710, 3210
29 45°
30 line CD
31 Isosceles (also right-angled)
32 never
33 13 cm²
34 2
35 105 cm²
36 76 cm
37 500 ml
38 900 ml
39 =
40 <
41

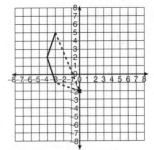

42 (3,–1) (4, 2) (3, 5)
43 March
44 13 °C
45 May
46 16 °C
47 20 °C
48 6 °C
49 12.75 °C
50 12 °C

Bond Maths Assessment Papers Stretch 9–10 years

30 Name the solid shape that has 4 triangular faces, 6 edges and 4 vertices. _____

31 Name the 3-D shape that has no vertices, 2 edges and 2 circular faces.

_____

4

32–33 A classroom is 7.5 m wide and 10 m long. Calculate the area and perimeter of this classroom.

Area = _____ m²

Perimeter = _____ m

2

The area of a rectangle is 32 cm. It is twice as long as it is wide.

34 What is the length of this rectangle? _____ cm

35 What is the width of this rectangle? _____ cm

2

A

B

36 Which scale shows the heavier weight, A or B? _____

37 What is the total weight of these two amounts? _____ kg

38 What is the difference in grams between these two weights? _____ g

3

39 Look at the first flag. Circle the flag that is a **rotation** of the first flag.

A   B   C   D

1

40 Look at the first triangle. Circle the triangle that is a **reflection** of the first triangle.

A   B   C   D

1

41 Write the coordinates for A.

(_____, _____)

42 Mark coordinate (−4, 3) on the grid and label it B.

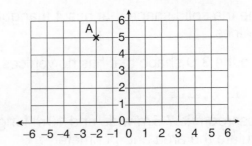

2

This chart shows the clothes sold in a shop in January.

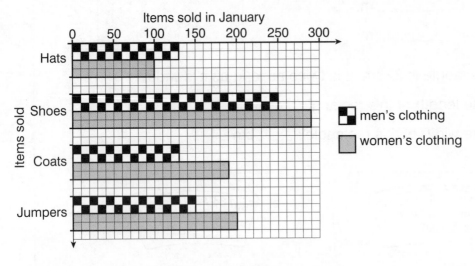

43 How many men's coats were sold? _____

44 How many more women's shoes were sold than men's shoes?

_____

45 How many jumpers were sold in total? _____

46 Is the following statement true or false? _____

"Hats were the only item that sold more for men than women."

4

These are Tom's scores in a daily spelling test over one week.
Monday→14   Tuesday→15   Wednesday→18   Thursday→14   Friday→19

47 What is Tom's mean average score? _____

48 What is Tom's median score? _____

49 What is Tom's mode score? _____

50 What is the range of his scores? _____

4

Mixed paper 3

1–5 These are the average depths of the deepest oceans and seas in the world.

Write each depth to the nearest 1000 m.

Ocean/Sea	Average depth (metres)	Rounded to nearest 1000 m
Atlantic Ocean	3926	_____
Caribbean Sea	2647	_____
Pacific Ocean	4028	_____
Indian Ocean	3963	_____
South China Sea	1652	_____

○ 5

Look at these decimal numbers.

    2.9   5.4   1.7   3.6

6–7 Which two decimal numbers have a difference of 2.5? _____ and _____

8–9 Which two decimal numbers total 9? _____ and _____

○ 4

10–13 This is a 'divide by 30 machine'. Write the missing numbers in the chart.

IN → [÷ 30] → OUT

IN	150	_____	360	450	_____
OUT	_____	8	_____	15	20

○ 4

14–15 Circle the two numbers that are prime numbers.

    29   39   49   59   69

○ 2

16 Write a multiple of 8 that would make this number sentence true.

$110 <$ _____ < 120

○ 1

17 Write a factor of 60 that would make this number sentence true.

$15 >$ _____ > 10

○ 1

Write the following fractions as percentages.

18 $\frac{9}{10} =$ _____ %   **19** $\frac{3}{5} =$ _____ %

○ 2

There are 16 pieces of fruit in a bowl, 4 apples and 12 oranges.

20 What fraction of the fruit are apples? _____

21 What fraction of the fruit are oranges? _____

22 What is the missing number in this sequence? Circle the correct answer.

41   50   60   71   _____   96

a 85   **b** 83   **c** 81   **d** 87

23 What is the rule or pattern for this sequence? Circle the correct answer.

0   2.5   5   7.5   10

a double the number   **b** halve the number   **c** add 0.5   **d** add 2.5

24–25 Write the missing numbers in this sequence.

_____   3550   3570   3590   3610   _____

26 Name the shape this net will make when it is folded. _____

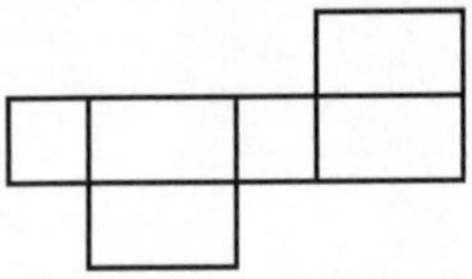

27 Measure this angle carefully with a protractor. _____°

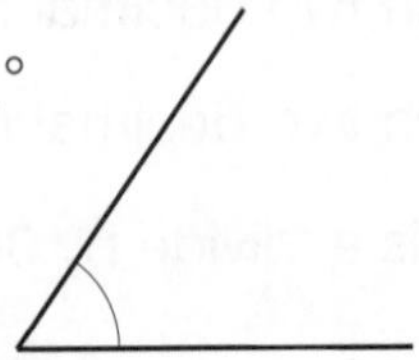

28 Circle the shape that is a regular polygon.

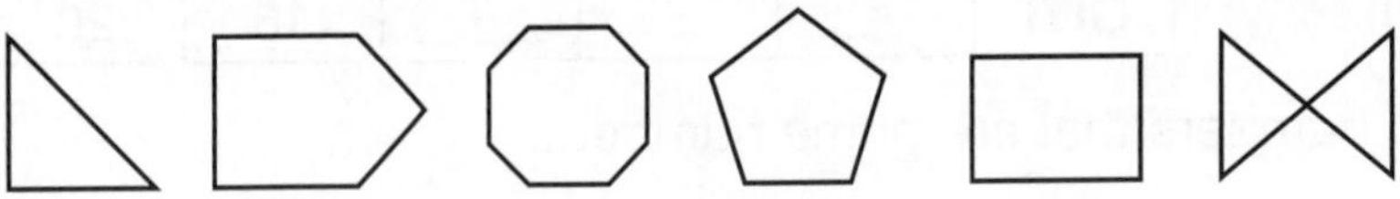

A   B   C   D   E   F

29–30 Draw two lines of symmetry on this shape.

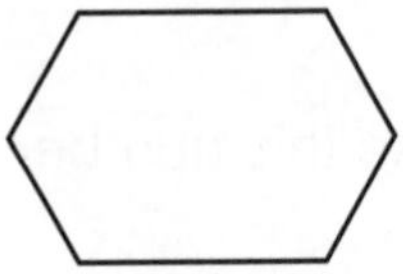

Calculate the length of the sides of these squares.

31

Area = 49 cm²

Length of side = _____ cm

32 □

Area = 9 cm²   Length of side = _____ cm   ② 2

33–34 What are the perimeter and area of a swimming pool that is seven metres wide and twelve metres long?

Perimeter = _____ m   Area = _____ m²   ② 2

Write the amount shown in each jug in millilitres.

35    **36**

_____ ml   _____ ml   ② 2

37 What is the difference between the amount of liquid in these two jugs?
_____ ml   ① 1

38 The liquid in these two jugs is poured into an empty bucket. How much liquid is in the bucket? _____ litres.   ① 1

39 Mark coordinates (−3, 5) on the grid and draw two straight lines to complete Shape A.

40 Mark coordinates (4, 0) on the grid and draw two straight lines to complete Shape B.

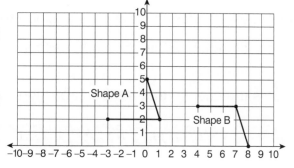

41 Circle the correct transformation of Shape A to Shape B.

Translation   Rotation   Reflection

42 Circle the coordinates that match one of the vertices of Shape A.

(2, 1)   (3, 3)   (−3, 0)   (0, 5)   (2, −3)   ④ 4

43 How many children are over 161 cm in height? _____

44 Which range of heights is the mode?

Circle the correct range.

130 cm or under   131 cm–140 cm

141 cm–150 cm   151 cm–160 cm

161 cm or over

45 How many children are 140 cm or less in height? _____

46 How many children are there in total in Class H? _____

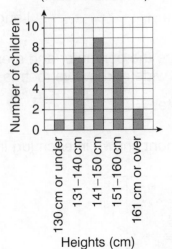

Heights of children in Class H
(to the nearest cm)

Number of children

Heights (cm)

4

There are 4 red, 2 green and 6 yellow balloons. One of the balloons bursts.

0   1

impossible   unlikely   even chance   likely   certain

47 What is the chance that the burst balloon was yellow? _____

48 What is the chance that the burst balloon was red? _____

49 What is the chance that the burst balloon was **not** green?

_____

50 What is the chance that the burst balloon was blue? _____

4

Now go to the Progress Chart to record your score!   Total   50

Mixed paper 4

1–4 Write the numbers at each position on this number line.

4   6

4

Complete these calculations.

5
$$\begin{array}{r} 29.86 \\ + 53.22 \\ \hline \\ \hline \end{array}$$

6
$$\begin{array}{r} 51.49 \\ - 19.78 \\ \hline \\ \hline \end{array}$$

This table shows the distance of flights from London to Rome and New York.

7 What is the distance of a **return** flight from London to Rome?
_____ km

	Rome	New York
London	1459 km	5557 km

8 How much further from London is New York than Rome?
_____ km

9 $0.75 \times 8 =$ _____

10 $160 \times 36 =$ _____

11 What is the smallest number that can be added to 450 to make it exactly divisible by 8? _____

12 In a survey of how children travelled to school, one third of the 357 children walked. How many children walked to school?
_____

13-14 Circle the two numbers that are a multiple of 7.

27   39   44   56   68   73   85   91

15-16 Write the missing pair of factors for 54.

(1, 54) (2, 27) (___, ___) (6, 9)

Circle the mixed number with the same value as the improper fraction.

17 $\frac{7}{2}$ $7\frac{1}{2}$ $3\frac{1}{7}$ $2\frac{1}{3}$ $3\frac{1}{2}$ $1\frac{2}{7}$

18 $\frac{12}{5}$ $2\frac{2}{5}$ $1\frac{2}{5}$ $6\frac{1}{5}$ $2\frac{2}{10}$ $2\frac{1}{5}$

19 What is $\frac{4}{5}$ of 25? _____

20 What is $\frac{2}{3}$ of 18? _____

21-22 In this sequence each number is half the previous number. Write the missing numbers.

112   ____   28   14   7   ____

2

2

2

1

1

2

2

2

2

2

33

23–24 Write the next two numbers in this sequence.

583   608   633   658   _____   _____

2

25 Calculate the size of angle *x* on this isosceles triangle.

_____ °

1

26 Complete this statement with **always**, **sometimes** or **never**.

Triangles are _____ symmetrical.

1

48°

x   *x*

27 Measure this angle carefully with a protractor.

_____ °

1

Calculate the area of the shaded shapes on this 1cm square grid.

28 _____ cm²   **29** _____ cm²

2

30 Which has the larger area, Room A or Room B? Room _____

31 Which has the longer perimeter? Underline the statement that is true.

Room A has the longer perimeter.

Room B has the longer perimeter.

The perimeters of Room A and B are the same length.

Room A   7 m

8 m

Room B   6 m

9 m

2

32–35 Write this set of measures in order, starting with the smallest.

0.28 m   82 cm   2.8 cm   82 mm

_____ _____ _____ _____

Smallest →

4

36–39 Plot these coordinates and join them in order to make a quadrilateral.
Label each point with a letter.
Draw a line from point D to point A.

A (1, 3)   B (−2, 6)

C (−5, 3)   D (−2, −5)

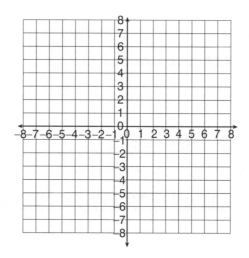

40 What is the name of this quadrilateral? _____

41 How many lines of symmetry are there on this shape? _____

42 Is the angle at (−2, −5) on this shape reflex, obtuse, acute or a right angle? _____

Look at this conversion chart.

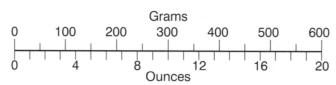

43 Approximately how many grams are there in 20 ounces? _____

44 Approximately how many ounces are there in 450 grams? _____

45–46 An old recipe for biscuits lists the amount of each ingredient in ounces. Use the chart to convert each amount to grams.

Butter   5 ounces → _____ grams

Flour   10 ounces → _____ grams

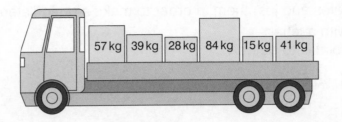

47 What is the mean weight of the boxes on this lorry? _____

48 What is the median weight of the boxes on this lorry? _____ ◯ 2

49–50 Another box weighing 30 kg is placed on the lorry.

What is the mean weight now? _____

What is the median weight now? _____ ◯ 2

Now go to the Progress Chart to record your score! **Total** ◯ 50

Mixed paper 5

Answer the following calculations:

1 $0.06 \times 100 =$ _____ **2** $23.1 \times 100 =$ _____ ◯ 2

3 $1806 \div 100 =$ _____ **4** $72 \div 100 =$ _____ ◯ 2

5 $4837 + 1596 =$ _____ **6** $23.5 + 16.9 =$ _____ ◯ 2

7 What is 50 430 take away 7800? _____

8 Add together 19 627 and 50 648. _____ ◯ 2

9 Divide 574 by 17. _____ ◯ 1

10 Apples cost £1.50 per kilogram. How many kilograms of apples can be bought for £12? _____ kg ◯ 1

11–12 Circle two numbers which, when multiplied together have the answer closest to 70.

8   17   9   23   6   3 ◯ 2

13 I am thinking of a number. If I multiply it by 6 and divide it by 42 the answer is 18. What is my number? _____ ◯ 1

14 $h^3 = 64$. What is the value of h? _____ ◯ 1

36

15 What is the next prime number after 13? _____

16–17 Write the missing factors of 57 in order.

$$57 \rightarrow 1 \ \underline{\quad} \ \underline{\quad} \ 57$$

Write these fractions as decimals.

18 $23\frac{4}{10} \rightarrow$ _____ **19** $17\frac{7}{10} \rightarrow$ _____

Change these mixed numbers to improper fractions.

20 $4\frac{2}{3} \rightarrow$ _____ **21** $2\frac{3}{8} \rightarrow$ _____

Continue these patterns for two more numbers.

22–23 56 65 74 83 _____ _____

24–25 391 388 385 382 _____ _____

Look at these shapes and answer the questions.

A   B   C   D   E

26 How many shapes are quadrilaterals? _____

27 How many shapes have no lines of symmetry? _____

28 How many shapes have a reflex angle inside? _____

29 How many shapes have obtuse angles inside? _____

30 The area of a square is 100 cm². What
is the length of one side of this square? _____cm

31–32 Calculate the area and perimeter
of this rectangle.

Area = _____ m²

Perimeter = _____ m

6 m

9.5 m

33 A football pitch is 95 m by 65 m. A white line is marked out around the
whole perimeter of the pitch. How long is the white line? _____ m

34–35 Look at the map and complete this bus timetable.

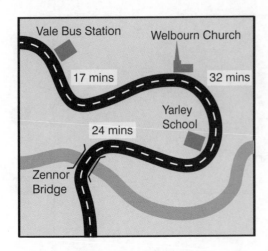

Vale Bus Station	11:50
Welbourn Church	_____
Yarley school	12:39
Zennor Bridge	_____

36 How long in total was the bus journey from Vale Bus Station to Zennor Bridge? _____ hour _____ minutes

37 The bus was 4 minutes early at Yarley School. What time did the bus arrive at Yarley School? _____

○ 4

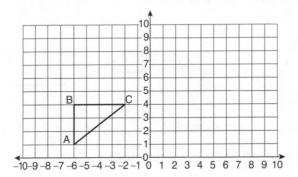

38–39 Write the missing coordinates for this triangle.

A →(_____, _____)   B →(_____, _____)   C → (−2, 4)

40 Circle the coordinates that can be found inside this triangle.

(−1, 2)   (−4, 6)   (3, −4)   (−5, 3)   (2, −2)

41 The triangle is rotated clockwise around point (−2, 4) so that vertex A is at (−5, 8). Where is the new position of vertex B? (_____, _____)

○ 4

The Venn diagram shows the food children in a class had in their lunch boxes after they had eaten their sandwiches.

42 How many children had fruit and cake but no yoghurt? _____

43 How many children only had a piece of fruit? _____

44 How many children had a yoghurt, fruit and cake in their box? _____

45 How many children had a yoghurt in their lunch box? _____

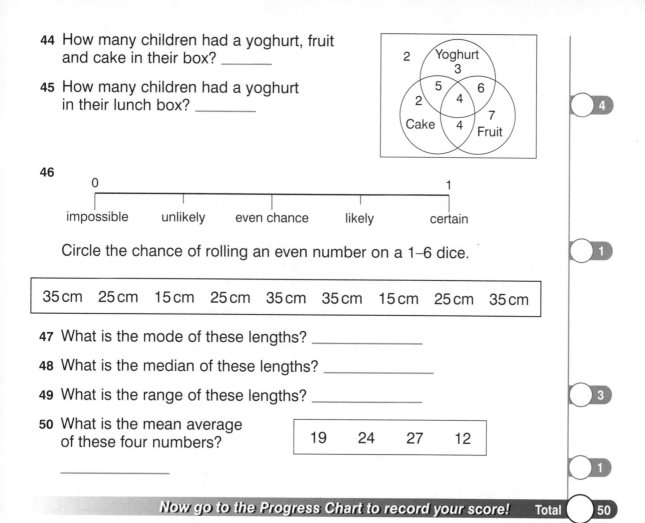

○ 4

46

```
0                                                    1
|-----------|-----------|-----------|-----------|
impossible  unlikely  even chance   likely      certain
```

Circle the chance of rolling an even number on a 1–6 dice.

○ 1

35 cm 25 cm 15 cm 25 cm 35 cm 35 cm 15 cm 25 cm 35 cm

47 What is the mode of these lengths? _____

48 What is the median of these lengths? _____

49 What is the range of these lengths? _____

○ 3

50 What is the mean average of these four numbers?

19   24   27   12

_____

○ 1

Now go to the Progress Chart to record your score!   Total ○ 50

Mixed paper 6

Circle the smallest number and underline the largest number in each group.

1–2 36.06   36.604   34.064   36.46   34.6

3–4 19.58   19.581   19.18   19.159   19.518

○ 4

5 How much more will it cost to buy the table than a chair? £_____

6 How much would it cost to buy a table and two chairs? £_____

£137.49   £89.95

39

7 Mr and Mrs Jays have £95. How much more do they need to buy the table? £_____

8 Mr and Mrs Jays decide to buy one chair. How much money will they have left from £95 if they buy one chair? £_____

9 The area of a rectangle is 234 cm². The shorter side is 9 cm. What is the length of the longer side? _____ cm

10 Ryan is 7 and his mother is four times older than he is. His grandfather is three times older than his mother. How old is Ryan's grandfather? _____ years

11 A school bus travels 40 km a day. The bus takes children to school on 5 days every week. There are 12 weeks in a term and 3 terms in a year. How far does the school bus travel in a year? _____

12 340 sandwiches are made for a wedding party, so that there are 4 sandwiches for each person. There will also be enough tomatoes for everyone to have 3 tomatoes each. How many tomatoes will be needed in total? _____

13–16 Write these numbers in the correct part of this Carroll diagram.

	A factor of 72	Not a factor of 72
A multiple of 8	_____	_____
Not a multiple of 8	_____	_____

24   36   48   60

17–18 Which two of these are equivalent to 20%? Circle the correct answers.

0.2 $\frac{2}{5}$ 0.5   0.02 $\frac{1}{5}$

19–20 Answer these.

$$\frac{3}{8} + \frac{1}{2} = \frac{\square}{\square} \qquad \frac{7}{10} - \frac{1}{5} = \frac{\square}{\square}$$

Write the missing number in each sequence.

21 2319   2279   2239   _____   2159   2119

22 10   8.8   _____   6.4   5.2

23 60   210   360   _____   660

24 What is the rule or pattern for this sequence? Circle the correct answer.

9999   9099   8199   7299   6399   5499

a − 100   **b** − 1000   **c** − 900   **d** − 1100

40

Calculate the missing angles. Do not use a protractor.

25

Angle A = _____°

26

Angle B = _____°

27

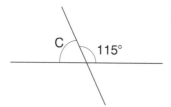

Angle C = _____°

28

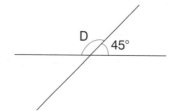

Angle D = _____°

29

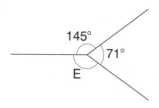

Angle E = _____°

[5]

Calculate the area and perimeter of this rectangle.

30 Area = _____ cm²

31 Perimeter = _____ cm

8 cm

3.8 cm

[2]

Calculate the area and total perimeter of this shaded shape.

32 Area = _____ m²

33 Perimeter = _____ m

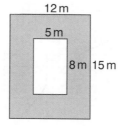

12 m
5 m
8 m 15 m

[2]

34 How much water must be added to 374.5 ml to make 1 litre?

_____

35 Circle the smallest amount.

     5 litres   1.5 litres   50 ml   0.5 litres   150 ml

[2]

Convert the weight shown on these scales to grams.

36
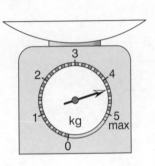
_____ g

37
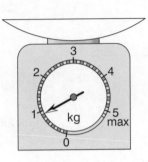
_____ g

38 Calculate this division. Write your answer in grams.

2.38 kg ÷ 7 = _____ g

39–42 Translate this shape so that it is 4 squares right and 5 squares up. Write the coordinates of each vertex of this translated shape.

(____ , ____) (____ , ____)

(____ , ____) (____ , ____)

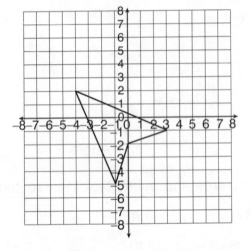

This graph shows the number of boys and girls in a school with birthdays in each month.

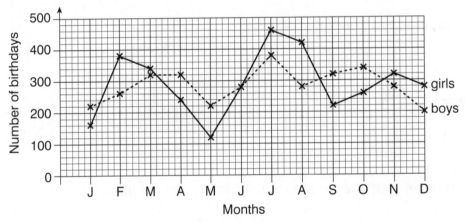

43 To the nearest 10, approximately how many girls were born in April?

_____

44 In which month were the same number of girls and boys born?

_____

45 How many more boys than girls were born in September?

_____

46 In which month is the difference in number of births between girls and boys the greatest? _____

4

These 1–9 digit cards are shuffled and placed face down in a row.

| 3 | 5 | 8 | 6 | 4 | 7 | 1 | 9 | 2 |

47 Underline the likelihood of picking a number less than 2.

impossible   poor chance   even chance   good chance   certain

48 Underline the likelihood of picking an odd number.

impossible   poor chance   even chance   good chance   certain

49 Underline the likelihood of picking a zero.

impossible   poor chance   even chance   good chance   certain

50 Which digit card is the median?_____

4

Now go to the Progress Chart to record your score!   Total   50

Mixed paper 7

Write each price to the nearest 10 p.

1 £187.25 → _____   2 £30.99 → _____

2

Write each price to the nearest pound.

3 £14.83 → _____   4 £25.49 → _____

2

Look at these numbers.

$$8.6 \quad 7.9 \quad 9.4 \quad 8.9 \quad 7.7$$

5–6 Which two numbers have a difference of 0.8? _____ and _____

7 What is the difference between the smallest and largest number? _____

8 What is the largest total that can be made by adding two of these numbers? _____

4

Complete these calculations:

9 $8204 \div 9 =$ _____   **10** $3756 \div 7 =$ _____

2

11 Divide nine hundred and sixty-two by twenty-six. Write your answer as in figures. _____

1

12 Which 3 **prime** numbers under 15 multiply to make 715?

_____ × _____ × _____ = 715

1

13 A right-angled isosceles triangle has two angles that are equal. What is the size of each angle? _____°

1

14–15 Circle the two numbers that are a multiple of 8.

$$84 \quad 96 \quad 108 \quad 128 \quad 133 \quad 142$$

2

16–17 Write the missing pair of factors for 92.

$$(1, 92) \quad (\text{\_\_\_\_}, \text{\_\_\_\_}) \quad (4, 23)$$

2

18 What percentage of this grid is light grey? _____

19 What fraction of this grid is dark grey? _____

2

20 Write < or > to make this number sentence true.

2.35 _____ $2\frac{3}{5}$

1

21 There are 30 children in Class R and 18 are girls. What percentage of the class are girls? _____%

1

22 What is the missing number in this sequence? Circle the correct answer.

$$40 \quad 50 \quad 70 \quad 100 \quad \text{\_\_\_\_} \quad 190$$

a 110   **b** 120   **c** 130   **d** 140

1

23–24 Write the missing numbers in this sequence

16   25   36   _____   64   _____   100   121

2

25 Write the next number in this sequence.

0   1   3   6   10   15   _____

1

26–29 Write the letter for each of these in the correct part of this Carroll diagram.

A cuboid   B cylinder   C tetrahedron   D triangular prism

	1 or more rectangular faces	No rectangular faces
1 or more triangular faces	_____	_____
No triangular faces	_____	_____

4

This is the plan of a house in a garden.

30 What is the area of the house? _____ m²

31 What is the area of the garden, not including the area of the house? _____ m²

House   8 m
12 m   Garden   15 m
30 m

32 A fence will be put round the whole garden. The fence panels are 1.5 m wide. How many fence panels will be needed? _____ fence panels

3

33 Draw a rectangle with an area of 64 squares and a perimeter of 40 squares.

1

34 Write the total length of these two bricks. _____ cm

35 What is the total length of five bricks? _____ cm

CM
0   1   2   3   4   5   6   7   8   9   10

2

45

Each of these parcels weighs a different amount.

Parcel B and C weigh 7 kg together.

Parcel A is double the weight of parcel B.

The total weight of all three parcels is 15 kg.

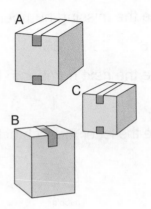

36 What is the weight of parcel A? _____ kg

37 What is the weight of parcel B? _____ kg

38 What is the weight of Parcel C? _____ kg

○ 3

39 This triangle has been rotated to make a pattern. Draw the next rotation in this sequence.

○ 1

40 This is a rectangle. Write in the missing coordinates. (_____ , _____)

○ 1

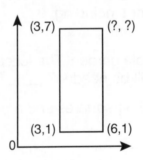

41 These shapes show a **reflection**. Draw in the mirror line that these shapes have been reflected in.

42 Circle the coordinates that are **not** on the mirror line.

(4, 4)   (3, −3)   (−2, −2)   (0, 0)

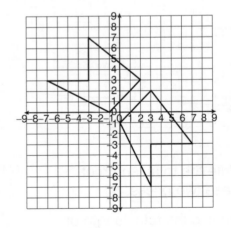

○ 2

This pie chart shows what Kate did with £4 of pocket money in one week.

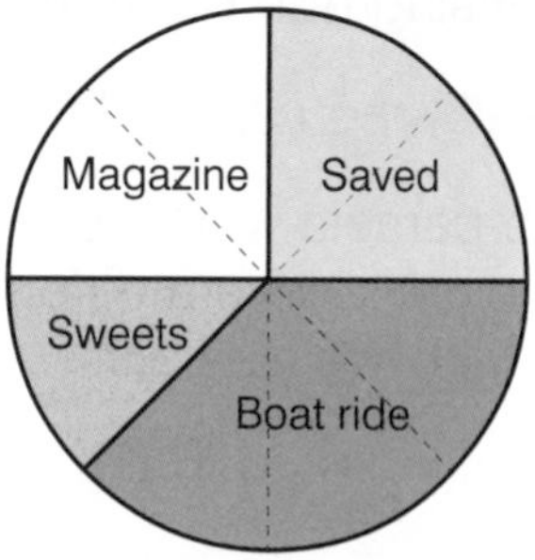

43 How much did Kate save? _____

44 How much did she spend on the boat ride? _____

45 How much did she spend on sweets?

_____

46 How much did she spend in total? _____ ◯ 4

47 If the mean average of two numbers is 8 and one number is 9, what is the other number? _____ ◯ 1

48 The total marks in a science test were 512. If the mean average mark was 32, how many children took the test? _____ ◯ 1

49 If the probability is 0.4 that it will not rain tomorrow, what is the probability that it will rain tomorrow? _____ ◯ 1

50 Write the probability, expressed as a percentage, of flipping 'heads' on a coin. _____ ◯ 1

Now go to the Progress Chart to record your score! **Total** ◯ 50

Mixed paper 8

1–4 Write this set of decimals in order to make this number sentence correct.

6.024   4.602   4.604   6.246

4.602 < 4.604 < 6.024 < 6.246 ◯ 4

Write the number shown on each abacus in words.

5

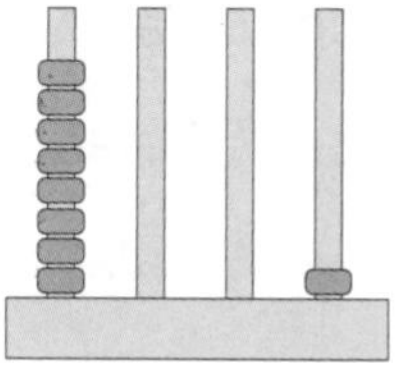

8001
eight thousand and one

6

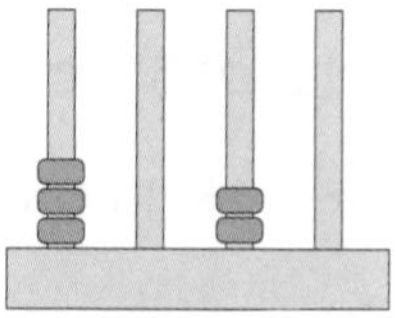

3020
three thousand and twenty ◯ 2

47

Write the missing number in each calculation.

7 $(34 - 25) + \underline{8} = 17$ 8 $\underline{27} + (19 + 6) = 52$ 2

9–10 Three parcels weigh 8.1 kg. One parcel weighs 3.5 kg and the other two parcels have a difference of 1 kg. Complete the missing weights of the other two parcels.

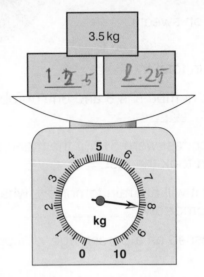

2

11 Which number between 60 and 70 has a remainder of 5 when it is divided by 8? _____   1

12 Eggs are sold in boxes of 12. A farmer collects 78 eggs in one day. How many egg boxes can be completely filled? _____   1

13 I am thinking of a number. I divide it by 7 and then multiply it by 50 and my answer is 450. What is my number? _____   1

14 A bag of potatoes weighs 2.5 kg. A supermarket shelf can hold a maximum weight of 30 kg. How many bags of potatoes can this shelf hold? _____   1

Are these statements true or false? Circle the correct answer.

15 A multiple of 9 is always an odd number.   True / False

16 When the digits of a number that is a multiple of 9 are added together, that total will always have 9 as a factor.   True / False

17 The number 30 has a total of 6 factors.   True / False

18 A square number always has an odd number of factors.   True / False   4

19–20 Circle the two cards that show more than $\frac{1}{2}$

8% $\frac{3}{8}$ 0.8   0.35 $\frac{3}{5}$ 38%

2

Circle the decimal number that is the same as each fraction.

21 $\frac{4}{10}$ 4   0.4   0.04   0.004   **22** $\frac{7}{100}$ 7   0.7   0.07   0.007

2

Look at this circle.

23 What fraction of this circle is shaded?

_____

24 What percentage of this circle is shaded?

_____

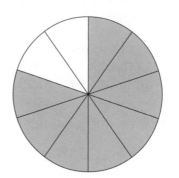

2

25 Write the first number in this sequence.

_____   10.6   11.2   11.8   12.4

1

26 What is the rule or pattern for this sequence? Circle the correct answer.

104   52   26   13   6.5

a halve the number **b** double the number

c take away 26   **d** add 13

1

27–28 Write the missing numbers in this sequence.

_____   2010   2310   2610   2910   _____

2

Look at this square.

29 Without using a protractor calculate the angle
marked x. _____

30 Which line is parallel to line AB? _____

31 What type of triangle is ABD? _____

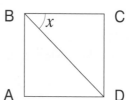

3

32 Write **always**, **sometimes** or **never** to make this sentence true.

A cube _____ has 2 square faces and 4 rectangle faces.

1

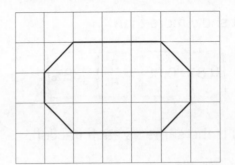

33 Calculate the area of the shape on this 1cm square grid.
_____ cm² 〔1〕

34 A rectangular lawn measures 7.5m by 4m. A packet of 'Seed and Feed' is enough for 15m². How many packets of 'Seed and Feed' would be needed for this lawn? _____ 〔1〕

Calculate the area and perimeter of this shape.

35 Area = _____ cm²

36 Perimeter = _____ cm 〔2〕

37 What is the difference, in millilitres, between the amount of water in these two jugs? _____ml

38 If these two jugs of water were poured together, how much **more** water would be needed to fill a 5 litre bowl? Write your answer in millilitres.
_____ml 〔2〕

Enter <, > or = to make each statement true.

39 40.5cm _____ 405mm   **40** 180g _____ 1.8kg 〔2〕

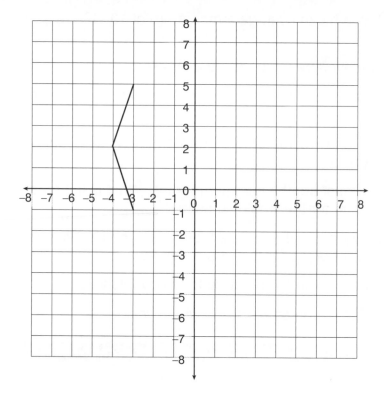

41 Mark coordinates (0, −2) on the grid. This is the fourth vertex of a quadrilateral. Draw two lines to complete this shape.

1

42 Draw a reflection of this shape, using the *y*-axis as the line of symmetry. Write the missing three coordinates of the reflected shape.

(0, −2) (_____, _____) (_____, _____) (_____, _____)

1

Mean average monthly temperature in Britain

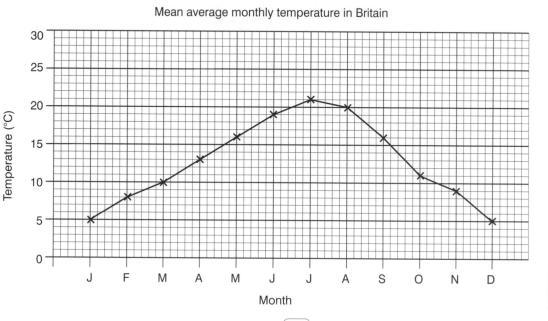

43 Which month has a mean average temperature of 10°C?

_____

44 What is the mean average temperature in April? _____

45 Which month has the same mean average temperature as September?

_____

46 What is the difference in temperature between the coldest month and the hottest month? _____

47 June, July and August are the summer months. What is the mean average temperature for the whole summer? _____

48 December, January and February are the winter months. What is the mean average temperature for the whole winter? _____

49 What is the mean average temperature for the whole year? _____

50 What is the median temperature for the whole year? _____

8